STEP BY STEP IN THE
JEWISH RELIGION

SONCINO PRESS
Books of Enduring Worth

STEP BY STEP

IN THE

JEWISH RELIGION

BY

RABBI ISIDORE EPSTEIN
B.A., Ph.D., D.Lit.
Principal of Jews' College, London

THE SONCINO PRESS
LONDON • NEW YORK

First Edition   1958
Second Impression 1959
Third   Impression 1965
Fourth Impression 1965
Second Edition   1968
Second Impression 1971
Third   Impression 1980
Fourth Impression 1993

Manufactured
in the United States of America

CONTENTS

Human Society – Rescuing our Fellow-Man from Danger – Provision of Livelihood. The Divine Owner – Charity – Concern for the feelings of the Poor – The Highest form of Charity – False Charity – Concern for the Property of Others. Righteousness towards Animals – Righteousness towards the rest of Creation.

The Height of Goodness – THOU SHALT LOVE THY NEIGHBOUR AS THYSELF – Love and the Machine of Human Society – Deeds of Lovingkindness – Special Deeds of Lovingkindness – (1) Bikkur Cholim (Visiting the Sick) – (2) Hachnasat Kallah (Dowering the Bride) – (3) Nichum Avelim (Comforting Mourners) – Love and our own Rights – General Acts of Love – Meaning of "Love your Neighbour" – Who is our Neighbour? – Brotherhood of Man – Love of the Stranger.

The True Son of Israel – The Good Pupil – How to Make and Keep the Mind Fit – The Enemies – Envy – Greed – Pride – The Fight – True Victory – The Greatest Danger – The Friends – The Greatest of Friends – The Greatest Thing in the World.

The Highest Perfection – The Holy Man-in-

PREFACE

This small book has been written in response to many requests from readers of my *Jewish Way of Life* for a similar work specially adapted to the needs of young people eager to know the "whys" and "wherefores" of the teachings of the Jewish Religion. The aim throughout has therefore been one of simplicity and directness. The result is a work which, although treating of the same theme as the earlier one, is entirely new alike in construction and presentation.

The plan of the work is indicated in the title : it leads the reader "step by step" through the essential teachings of the Jewish religion until he discovers for himself much of the wealth of meaning which Judaism holds for him and for the conduct of his daily life.

From Hillel's famous principle, "What is hateful to you do not unto your fellow", the work proceeds logically through details of the laws of JUSTICE, RIGHTEOUSNESS, and LOVE to the goal which is HOLINESS – the quality which makes for a good, useful and serene life. Each step is explained by means of simple illustrations, and illumined by appropriate quotations from the Bible and the Talmud as well as from other sources.

The moral duties and the religious observances – the daily ritual, the Sabbath, Festivals, and Fasts – as well as the fundamental beliefs of Judaism are described and interpreted and so interlinked with each other as to form a harmonious whole.

Although essentially a book for young people it has also a meaning and significance for all those who wish to gain a better insight into Judaism.

The Appendix, at the end of the volume, giving the Hebrew original of the Biblical and Talmudic passages appearing in the work, has been prepared by Miss Ruth Lehmann, A.L.A., to whom I wish to express my cordial thanks. I am also indebted to Mrs. J. Woolf for reading the proofs, and to Mr. S. M. Bloch, the Director of the Soncino Press, for supervising the publication of this work through all the various stages.

Sivan 5718   I.E.
June 1958

Chapter 1

STEP BY STEP

The Teacher Hillel

About two thousand years ago, there lived in the Land of Israel a famous Rabbi, named Hillel. He was a saintly man, very meek and patient. He never lost his temper with anyone. People, who wished to try his patience, played jokes on him. They would come to him with the most stupid questions to see if they could annoy him, but they always went away wiser than they came; for Hillel knew how to turn a silly question into a useful lesson.

No wonder Hillel was respected by both Jews and non-Jews. One day a heathen approached the Rabbi saying that he would embrace Judaism if he could be taught the Torah while he stood on one foot! Hillel was not shocked at the man's impudence, and did not rebuke him for it. On the contrary, he allowed him to feel that he had a right to ask for an explanation, in a few words, of the teaching of the Jewish religion. And indeed, by his reply, Hillel showed his own greatness.

There were two obvious answers Hillel could have given to the heathen.

The first was to tell him that the Jewish religion teaches us to believe in One God. This is the answer any other man might have given. But Hillel knew better. He knew he had to deal with a non-Jew who believed that there were many gods; one god who made the heaven, another god who made the earth, and another the mountains, and yet another the sea, and so on. As such the heathen would surely not have understood that there could be only One God, who made the heaven and the earth and everything in the world.

Besides, brought up to worship gods made of wood or stone, the non-Jew who questioned Hillel would have found it difficult to understand how it was possible to worship a God who can neither be seen with the eyes, nor touched with the hands. To make the heathen grasp the difference between the One God and the many gods would thus have meant giving long and difficult explanations; and that certainly could not have been done while he stood on one foot.

The second way Hillel could have answered the heathen was to quote from the Book of Leviticus the words, "You shall love your neighbour as yourself."[1] This commandment of the Jewish religion, known as the "Golden Rule," might have been easier for the non-Jew to understand. It is a rule of great value and yet so

simple, so human. "Love" and "neighbour" are
words which need no explanation. The heathen surely
had parents whom he loved; and perhaps also a wife
and children whom he loved. And he must have known
what a "neighbour" meant—the men and women he
met in his daily life. But Hillel knew that there was
something in the command which the heathen could
not have grasped. Everywhere around him there was so
much hate and spite that the ready retort the heathen
could have given to Hillel's advice might have been
something like this: "Yes, my dear Rabbi, all this talk
about loving my neighbour as myself sounds strange
to me. It is sheer nonsense. How can I love my neighbour whom I dislike or, more important, who may dislike me! You cannot be really serious when you expect
me to accept a religion which demands such an impossible thing of me."

Hillel knew and understood the heathen well. He did
not mention to him the belief in One God. Neither did
he ask him to love his neighbour. All that he said to
him was simply: "What is hateful to you, do not do
unto your fellow.[2] The rest is explanation."

Hillel's Easy Lesson
This seems to mean less than the "Golden Rule of
Love," but in reality it meant much more; because it
was the first lesson in good behaviour. It was a simple

lesson which even the heathen would find easy to learn, and not too difficult to practise. Whenever in future he was tempted to do wrong to his neighbour, he need only ask himself: "How would I like it if my neighbour did this to *me*?" He need only put this question to himself, and the answer would be clear: "I certainly would not like it." If he asked himself the question with sincerity, he would have to accept the answer, and refuse to carry out his evil purpose. He would then see no point in hating his neighbour, and would therefore cease to hate him. This would give him a good start towards learning to love his neighbour. Thinking further, he would find that he was not likely to love his neighbour if he did not love God who commanded us to love our neighbours. This would at last make him a follower of the Jewish religion.

By giving the non-Jew this answer, Hillel has given an important lesson in behaviour to all the world: to all those Jewish men and women who want to be true to their religion; and to the whole of mankind.

The Jewish religion is not the special property of a few chosen families or tribes. Neither can a single people claim, all to itself, such a precious gift as the Jewish religion. When it was the will of God to give to human beings His Torah, which teaches the way of good conduct and decent behaviour, He also offered it, so we are told, to other nations, but no people, apart from the

Jews, was ready to accept it. The commands of the
Torah were regarded by the other peoples as a burden
too heavy to carry. They interfered too much with their
way of life, their petty hatreds, quarrels, fights, and
evil desires. An old legend tells us that when God
offered the Torah to the children of Esau, the first
question they asked was: "What is written in this
Torah?" When they heard that it contained the commandment, "You shall not murder," they immediately
turned down the offer; for they could not imagine how
they could do away with murder. And so all the other
peoples, in turn, in those days of old, found in the
Torah one thing or another they were not prepared to
accept. The only people prepared to accept all that the
Torah ordered, and to carry out all its commands,
was the Jewish people. And so the Torah was given to
our people. But in reality the Jewish religion belongs,
in a sense, to the whole world and concerns all mankind. Its aim is to make people hate each other less and
less, and feel more and more friendly, until one day,
they all love each other as brothers.

The times we live in make it specially important for
all of us, young and old, to take the lesson of Hillel to
heart. Things have changed much since God gave the
Torah to the Jewish people and since the days of Hillel,
who taught his generation how to live and act in the
spirit of the Torah.

Nowadays the peoples of the world still refuse to live as God wants them to live, and as the Torah teaches them to live. There is still much hatred and quarrelling, suffering and cruelty; and nations are more afraid of one another than ever before. This makes it all the more the duty of every Jewish man and woman, boy and girl, to show to the world that they still belong to that ancient people which alone, about four thousand years ago, willingly accepted the Torah, and agreed to live by its laws and commandments. All the more is it the duty of each one of us to set an example to others of that kind of good life that is pleasing to both God and man.

The necessary lessons for this kind of good life are not too difficult. They can best be learnt step by step.

What these steps are will be explained in the chapters that follow.

Chapter II

THE FIRST STEP—JUSTICE

The Easiest Step

The first step leading to a good Jewish life is Justice. In Hebrew it is called *Mishpat*. Justice is the easiest step, and its rules present little difficulty.

Justice means, "Not doing unto others what is hateful to ourselves," exactly what Hillel told the non-Jew: nothing more, but nothing less. In other words, it means not doing any harm or injury to our neighbour. This may be simple enough, but it has the great merit of making things safe. Remove justice, and society will soon go to rack and ruin, and cease to exist altogether.

Justice is therefore the least we may expect from any decent human being. No decent person in his senses will take a spanner and throw it into a revolving machine that turns out good and useful things. He knows quite well that the spanner, however small, will cause a good deal of mischief. Soon the cogs will break, the belts snap in two, and the whole machine be brought to a standstill and made a total wreck. This is what happens when a man disobeys the rule of Justice, and does

7

not hesitate to harm his neighbour. He throws a spanner into the most important machine in the world, the machine of human society in which we all depend, and of which each one of us forms a part. By injuring one portion of it, this man injures the machine as a whole, and by his thoughtlessness brings about misery and trouble, strife and confusion.

THE THREE DEMANDS OF JUSTICE

It is for this reason that the Jewish religion insists that the first thing a man must learn is to practise Justice. If you read the Bible and the works of the Rabbis carefully, you will find that Justice holds the first place in their teachings about human behaviour. Justice demands of each one of us three things:

1. It demands that we shall respect the life of others.
2. It demands that we shall respect the property of others.
3. It demands that we shall respect the feelings of others.

DEMAND NO. I — RESPECT FOR HUMAN LIFE

Justice demands that we shall respect the life of others.
This means that we must not destroy the life of any human being. Respect for human life is what distinguishes civilized men from barbarians. Among barbarians life is cheap; among civilized men life is precious.

Barbarians look upon murder with indifference; civilized men look upon murder with horror. Even to-day,
when the world is full of violence and cruelty beyond
imagination, we still shudder when we learn from newspapers that a murder has been committed.

This respect for human life, which has now become
the rule among civilized people, the world has learned
from the Jews. Four thousand years ago it was considered the right thing for men to kill each other for
the slightest reason. A man coveted his neighbour's possessions, his house, his field, his ox or ass, and he
thought nothing of killing him so as to get them, if
he was strong enough to do so. Then came the Jewish
religion, with its Ten Commandments, and proclaimed
"Thou shalt not murder." This immediately declared
murder a crime. The Jewish religion was the first to
teach that life is a precious gift from God, and that to rob
a man of his life is to be guilty of a monstrous offence
for which the most severe penalty must be paid.
"Whosoever sheddeth man's blood, by man shall his
blood be shed; for in the image of God hath He made
man" (Genesis, 9, 6). These words from the Bible are
clear and precise. Every man has been made in the
image of God. To kill any man is therefore to destroy
something divine, and it is a crime which deserves to
be punished with the most severe penalty the law can
impose.

The purpose of the law which requires that the murderer shall pay with his own life for taking the life of another man, is not revenge. Its object is to prevent people giving away to murderous feelings. It is true that the fear of death does not stop murder altogether, but at least it serves as a check to most people, and thus helps to make the world a safer place in which to live.

Indeed, the very idea of revenge for murder is opposed to Judaism. In olden times, and even to the present day, among barbarous tribes, if a man killed another even by accident, it was the duty of the nearest relative of the man who was killed to act as an "avenger of blood," and to kill the slayer. All this has been forbidden by the Jewish religion. He who killed a man by accident was given the full protection of the law from the fury of the nearest relative. He was taken under guard to one of the cities of refuge that were specially set up in ancient Israel for the purpose, and he had to stay there until such time as it was supposed that the nearest relative would give up all thoughts of vengeance.

Even if the murder was committed deliberately, the nearest relative had no right to take the law into his own hands. The criminal had to be brought before the Court, where he had to receive a fair trial before sentence could be passed on him. From this we see again

how precious in the eyes of the Jewish law is the life
of every human being. No person accused of murder
could be sentenced to death, unless there was definite
proof that he had planned and committed the crime
with deliberate intention. At least two reliable wit-
nesses had to give evidence that they had actually
seen him commit the murder, and that he was fully
aware of the serious nature of the wicked deed he was
about to carry out. If there was no such evidence, the
murderer would escape the death penalty. In such a
case he could at most be sentenced to imprisonment
for life. No confession was extorted from him to send
him to death; and torture, that was practised everywhere in non-Jewish lands, and still is in some countries even to-day, was always unthinkable in Jewish
law.

Respect for human life forbids a man to destroy the
life of another innocent person even in order to save
his own life. A story is told in the Talmud of a man who
was threatened by the governor of his town with death
if he did not kill a certain person. That man came
before a Rabbi, whose name was Raba, and asked what
he was to do. "Let the governor kill you," was the reply
of the Rabbi, "rather than you should kill the other
person. What makes you think that your blood is red-
der than his?" Of course if we are attacked it is only
right that we should defend ourselves, but on no account

may a man save his own life by taking the life of another innocent human being.

Personal Injuries

Respect for human life not only forbids killing a person, but injuring anyone in health or limb. To inflict wounds or injuries upon our fellow-man is a crime. The penalty for this crime is not death, but the payment, as compensation, of a certain sum of money fixed by the Court, which varies with the nature of the injury.

This law of compensation is clearly laid down in the Book of Exodus, Chapter 21, verses 18-19.

"If two men fight and one man injures the other man with a stone or with his fist, and he does not die but keeps to his bed, and then rises again and walks about upon his staff, then shall the man who smote him be free, but he must pay for the loss of time and cause him to be thoroughly healed."

The Meaning of "Eye for Eye"

This payment of compensation is set forth in another place in the Bible by the words, "Eye for eye, tooth for tooth, hand for hand, foot for foot, burning for burning, wound for wound, stripe for stripe" (Exodus 21, 23-24). These words should not be misunderstood. They do not mean that if a man puts out the eye of another man, his own eye should be put out; or that if he knocks out the other's tooth, his own tooth should be knocked out, and so on. You may indeed sometimes hear it said that the Jewish religion approves of the principle, "tit for tat," and teaches revenge. This is completely wrong. The words "eye for eye" were never meant to be taken in this sense. This would not only contradict the law of compensation for injuries laid down in the verses mentioned above; it would be also against the whole spirit of the Jewish religion, which as we shall see later on, forbids vengeance of any kind.

There is no doubt that words "eye for eye" mean nothing more than that the value of an eye shall be paid for the loss of an eye; and this is how the Jewish teachers and Jewish Courts have always understood the phrase. In other words, it repeats the law of compensation for injuries already given. The phrase, "eye for eye," however, was used to express this law of compensation for two reasons.

1. The phrase "eye for eye" is intended to impress upon the offender the terrible nature of the crime of injuring a person and the extent of his duty to make good the damage. It should also help in a way to restrain angry men and teach them to control their tempers.

2. The phrase "eye for eye" also serves to limit the punishment that may be inflicted on a man for

the harm he has done to his neighbour. Its message is: You may not inflict upon a man a punishment out of proportion to the crime he has done. Eye for eye, tooth for tooth, so much punishment may be expected, but no more—not, for example two eyes for one eye, or ten teeth for one tooth.

A little over a hundred years ago, hanging was the punishment for small thefts even in England. People were sentenced to death for the most trivial offences, such as the snaring of a pheasant or the burning of a hay-rick. As late as 1833, we are told, "Sentence of death was passed on a child of nine who poked a stick through a pane of glass in a shop-front and stole some pieces of paint worth two-pence." We have only to recall these cruelties practised not so very long ago, to understand the true significance of the warning given by the Bible about four thousand years ago that on no account was the offender to undergo a punishment greater than his crime deserved.

Attacking a Person

Respect for human life forbids us also to attack any human being. To strike a person, even without causing him any injury, is, in the eyes of the Jewish Law, regarded as a crime. Moreover, merely to lift a hand against another person without actually striking him, is branded by the Jewish religion as a crime. "He who lifts up his hand against his fellow although he does not strike him is called a wicked man."[1] This is a saying of our Rabbis which we should bear well in mind in all our dealings with others.

Protection against Accidents

To do no harm or injury to our neighbour is not enough. Respect for human life demands that we should do all that is in our power to see that no harm comes to others through our neglect or carelessness. In Bible times, the houses had flat roofs which were put to use. People used to walk about, take their meals, and perform all kinds of household work on them. For this reason the Bible commanded that every house must have a parapet or fence built round the roof to prevent people from falling off :

"If you build a new house, you shall make a parapet for your roof, in order that you may not bring the guilt of blood upon your house, in case any man shall fall from thence" (Deuteronomy 22, 8).

This Biblical law, as the teachers of the Jewish religion have pointed out, is given only as an example of what must be done to remove every possible source of danger to the health and well-being of our fellows. They therefore also forbade us to keep in the house a dangerous dog unleashed, or an unsafe ladder. It is likewise forbidden to throw into the street fruit peelings or anything on which people are likely to slip and injure themselves. These laws ordained several thousands of years ago by the Jewish religion inspired the regulations requiring, for example, the fencing of dangerous machinery, which have been made only in recent times for the protection of workmen.

DEMAND NO. 2 — RESPECT FOR PROPERTY

Justice demands that we shall respect the property of others. This means that we must not take away from people anything which properly belongs to them.

This respect for the property of others is another mark of distinction between civilized people and barbarians. Among barbarians property is not safe; among civilized men property is, on the whole, protected. Here, too, it was the Jewish religion which showed the way when it announced about four thousand years ago, "Thou shalt not steal."

Theft and Robbery

This commandment, which is the Eighth of the Ten Commandments, is repeated with some additional detail in other parts of the Bible and is fully explained in the teachings of the Rabbis. There we see that any action which serves to deprive a man of his possessions by unfair means, is a crime. It is also a crime to do anything which serves to encourage theft. For this reason the Jewish religion forbids us to purchase an article that has been stolen, or even to accept a gift or charity from a person who is known to be a thief. The crime of those who by their action encourage theft or robbery is well illustrated by the Rabbis in their parable, "Not the mouse is the thief, but the hole through which it gets in and out is the thief." Likewise, it is the man who enables the thief to get rid of his stolen property at a profit, who is the real thief. Without him the thief would often see no point in stealing.

It is also forbidden to steal even for a joke. You have only to begin stealing for a joke to find yourself developing unhealthy habits, and in the end you will steal in earnest. It is also forbidden to play the part of a Robin Hood, robbing one person in order to help another.

Misappropriation

Respect for the property of others forbids all practices known as "misappropriation". Among such ugly practices, often passed over, but considered in the eyes of the Jewish religion to be robbery, are the following:

1. To keep an article we have found without trying to discover the owner.

2. To use something belonging to another person without his consent, unless it is certain that he would not object.

3. To make use of something entrusted to us for safe keeping.

4. To make wrong use of something borrowed or hired.

5. To lend to another something lent to us.

All these practices, examples of which will rapidly spring to mind, seem to many people too trivial and too commonplace to be condemned. Yet the Jewish religion takes a serious view of them all. They all amount to a violation of the respect which we must have for the property of our fellow-man.

"Removal of a Landmark"

Another common offence, which the Jewish religion strictly condemns, is known as *hassagat gevul*, "removal of a landmark." This offence is based on the prohibition laid down in Deuteronomy 19, 14, and 27, 17, against removing the landmark between two estates, for this act will in the end deprive one neighbour of part of his estate; and the term *hassagat gevul* has come to mean any unfair competition which injures a man's business, or takes away his usual customers. He who is guilty of such a practice is branded by the Jewish Law as "a wicked man."

Business Honesty

Respect for the property of others forbids all kinds of cheating and fraud in business:

> "If you sell anything to your neighbour or buy anything from your neighbour, you shall not defraud one another" (Leviticus 25, 14).[2]

It is therefore forbidden to sell things at a high and unfair price, or to take advantage of a man's ignorance of the market value of an article, and make him sell it to us at a low price.

It is also forbidden to deceive a purchaser as to the quality, weight or measure of the goods sold:

> "You shall do no wrong in judgment, in yard measurement, in weight, or in (any other kind of) measure. Just balances, just weights shall you have" (Leviticus 19, 35–6).[3]

This concern for honesty in business dealings, shown by the Bible, was largely unknown in the ancient world. The Jewish communities of old, following the lead of the Bible, had special inspectors to see that these rules were carried out. This control of prices, weights and measures, has now to some extent become the rule in the more civilized countries. Yet, despite this general acceptance of Jewish practice, the world is still a long way from the standard set by the Jewish religion; for apart from those goods which are under government control, sellers may charge whatever price they can get. The Jewish religion, however, does not allow for any exceptions. It forbids all overcharging, however small; and, where the overcharge amounts to one-sixth or more, it gives the person overcharged the right to demand satisfaction. If a shopkeeper, for example, charges six-pence for an article worth only fivepence, the buyer can reclaim from him the extra penny; if he charges over sixpence, the buyer can return the article to him and ask for all his money back.

There are many other rules of Jewish law, which protect the interests of both buyer and seller against any dishonesty, and which show how particular the Jewish religion is about the respect we must have for the property of other people. Today, unfortunately, in spite of all the efforts of governments to stamp out dishonesty in business, a good deal of fraud and cheating goes on. Shortages of any commodity in particular always give opportunities for dishonest dealings, and unscrupulous people do not hesitate to take advantage of them. For the Jew, however, his duty is clear. It is to keep his hands clean from all fraudulent practices, however wide-spread they may be. He must remember that to commit the smallest fraud is to sin against God and human

society. "For all who do such things are an abomination
to the Lord thy God" (Deuteronomy 25, 16). Today
as ever the testing-rule for him remains the same—it is
the test of Hillel: "What is hateful to you, do not do
unto others." Whenever the Jew is in doubt whether or
not a certain business deal is fair and honest, he has
only to put this test to himself to find the right answer.
If he is the seller, he has simply to imagine that he is
the buyer; if he is the buyer, he has simply to imagine
that he is the seller. He will then easily find out for
himself how to act in a way that is just and proper
in the eyes of God and men.

Payment of Wages

Respect for the property of others forbids holding back
from our fellow-men what is due to them. It is therefore forbidden to make a workman wait for his wages.

> "The wages of him that is hired shall not remain
> with you all night until the morning."
>
> (Leviticus 19, 13)⁴

As soon as the wages are due, they properly belong to
the workman, and to keep them back for any time is to
rob him of his possessions. Besides, the workman often
depends on his earnings to buy food for himself and
his family, and if he is not paid promptly he is likely
to suffer hardship.

"In his day you shall give him his wages, neither shall the sun go down upon it, for he is poor and his life depends on it" (Deuteronomy 24, 15).

This consideration for the workman, shown by the Jewish religion about four thousand years ago, is only now beginning to be recognized by the world at large. Respect for the property of others demands that the workman should be paid a fair living wage. What the worker brings in the performance of his work is his property. His sweat, his time, his skill, his toil—all these belong to him alone, and the master has no right to use them for his own benefit without making a proper payment in return. For this reason, in accordance with the Jewish law, wages have to be fixed in a manner which will enable the worker to enjoy a decent standard of living. To do less is to rob the worker of his possessions. This crime is described in the Bible as "oppression," and is classed with robbery.

"Thou shalt not oppress thy neighbour, nor rob him" (Leviticus 19, 13).[5]

Oppression of workmen has been going on throughout history. It is only necessary to read, for example, J. L. Hammond's *The Town Labourer,* or about the life of Lord Shaftesbury, to discover the incredible oppression of children and adults by slave-driving employers that existed in England as late as the nineteenth century. Yet from the earliest days the Bible brought workers under its protection. It is only in recent times that the conditions of workers have begun to improve and that a "fair wage" has become an accepted principle of common life.

The prohibition against holding back what is due is not limited to wages. It is also sinful to delay in returning borrowed things, or in paying rent for premises, or for other hired things. It is likewise wrong not to pay accounts promptly when they are due; and to borrow money and not to repay it is the mark of a "wicked man."

"The wicked man borrows and pays not back."

(Psalm 37, 21)

Honesty in Work

Respect for the property of others demands, on the other hand, that the worker shall carry out his work with honesty. The worker who deliberately slackens, lowers his output, scamps his work, or is unpunctual, is in a sense guilty of robbery, because he does not respect that which is due to another man—his employer. He must also resist the temptation to carry off remnants of material used in connection with his work. They may be mere trifles to which he thinks he is entitled, as his "perks," but in reality they belong to the employer, and the worker must not take them without permission.

No Exceptions

These laws allow of no exception and must be observed in all our dealings with our fellow beings, whether Jews or non-Jews.

"Fraud, craft, all sorts of tricks, delusion and deceit towards non-Jews are forbidden. The teachers of old have said, 'It is forbidden to misrepresent anything to anybody, including the heathen'" (Moses Maimonides).

In fact the teachers of Israel about two thousand years ago declared that to deceive a non-Jew is worse than to deceive a Jew, because, in addition to deceiving a fellow-man, such an action brings the Jewish religion into bad repute and is a profanation of the Name of God—*Chillul Hashem.*

Injury to Property

Respect for the property of others also demands that we should treat the property of our fellow-man with the same care as we do our own.

"Let the property of your neighbour be as dear to you as your own" (Ethics of the Fathers 2, 17).[7]

We must therefore be careful that no harm should

come to the property of other people through our negligence or carelessness. Examples of such carelessness are far too common to need mention. Indeed, to take extreme precautions in such matters is, in the eyes of the Jewish religion, the mark of a holy man. Here, too, the test is that of our teacher Hillel: "What is hateful to you, do not do unto others."

Respect for Public Property

Respect for the property of others applies to public no less than to private property. This is a principle which people, otherwise honest, are tempted to ignore. There are a large number of men and women who would not think of picking the pockets of an individual, and yet do not consider it a crime to travel in a bus or train without paying the fare, or to "wangle" in matters of taxation. Yet it has been the law from the very early days of the Jewish religion that to defraud the public is at least as grave a sin as to rob a private person, and is as strictly forbidden.

DEMAND NO. 3 – RESPECT FOR FEELINGS

Justice demands that we shall respect the feelings of others. This means that we must avoid doing anything which may wound or hurt the feelings of our fellow man. "Man's one right," it has been said, "is to be a man"; and the Jewish religion insists that every human being should be treated with gentleness and consideration as a person, and not as a mere machine or thing.

There are various ways in which other people's feelings may be hurt:

(i) We can hurt their feelings by SLANDER.

(ii) We can hurt their feelings by INSULT.

(iii) We can hurt their feelings by DECEPTION.

(iv) We can hurt their feelings by ILL-WILL.

All such actions are sinful and contrary to the teachings of the Jewish religion, which demands that we shall respect the feelings of our fellow men as much as our own.

"Let the honour of your fellow be as dear to you as your own" (Ethics of the Fathers 2, 15).[8]

(i) SLANDER

The worst of the sins in this class is slander. In Hebrew slander is known as *leshon hara*, "the evil tongue." Slander, whether spoken against a Jew or a non-Jew, is a wicked sin. Nothing is more precious to a man than his good name. Everything depends upon his good name, and the good opinion people have of him. Everything, from his standing in society to his very livelihood. Destroy his good name, give him a bad character, and you may ruin him. Slander him, and you may be slaying him with your "evil tongue." For this reason slander is regarded in the eyes of the Jewish religion as a crime almost as foul as murder. We must therefore refuse to have anything to do with slander, as we would with murder. We must not only abstain from speaking slander; we must also resist the temptation to listen to slander.

> " 'You shall not take up a false report' (Exodus 23, 1)—that is, you shall not accept slanderous tales."
>
> (Talmud)

"Dust of the Evil Tongue"

The Bible warns us over and over again to keep away from slander. The Rabbis of the Talmud, who were very sensitive to all evildoing, interpreted the sin of slander in very wide terms. Slander, as they understood it, meant not only mischievous talk, spoken with the intention of blackening a man's name. Any "catty" remark, or unkind comment, was also regarded by these teachers of the Jewish religion as slander.

To this kind of slander the Rabbis gave the name, "the dust of the evil tongue."[9] A small particle of dust can be safely ignored, but when it is allowed to settle and is joined by other particles the effect is harmful. The same is true of the "dust of the evil tongue." You have only to indulge in it, and before long you will have spoiled your friend's reputation.

Furthermore, like dust, this kind of slander is difficult to avoid. We all raise the "dust of the evil tongue" in our daily conversation, tittle-tattle, and gossip, without realising that we are doing so. All the more is it our duty to guard our tongue from the sin of slander in any of its forms, however mild. All the more is it necessary for us to pay heed to the advice of the Psalmist:

"Who is the man that delights in life,
    And loves many days so that he may see good?
    Keep your tongue from evil, and your lips from
    speaking guile" (Psalm 34, 13–14).[10]

Here too our test must be that of Hillel: "What is hateful to you, do not do unto others."

Another offence which is regarded as "the dust of the evil tongue" is to reveal anyone's carefully-kept secret. This, of course, does not apply where the secret is one that is kept for the purpose of doing harm.

(ii) INSULT

Respect for feelings demands that we shall pay every consideration to the feelings of others. It is therefore forbidden to put a man to shame in the presence of other people. To put a man to shame in public is the worst insult we can inflict on him. You will have noticed that when a man is put to shame, his face changes colour. To cause this change of colour is considered to be like the shedding of blood.

"Wronging with Words"

Respect for the feelings of others demands that we should refrain from passing any remark that would hurt the feelings of our fellow men. It is therefore forbidden, for example, to remind a man of any offence he has once committed, and for which he has either paid the penalty or repented. It is also forbidden to remind a man of his lowly origin. Particular care must be taken in this respect in our dealings with strangers. Strangers are specially sensitive to the slightest of offensive words, It is therefore forbidden to refer to them in their presence as "aliens," or "foreigners," or "refugees." Insults of this kind are described by our teachers as "wronging with words." It is also considered as wronging with words to raise false expectations in a man. An example of this kind of wronging with words is to go into a shop and ask the price of an article without any intention of making a purchase.

(iii) DECEPTION

Respect for the feelings of others demands that we shall keep clear of all lying or deception. To lie to our

fellow man or to deceive him in any way is to offend
his honour and to wound his feelings as a human being.
It is therefore forbidden to tell an untruth to any person, whether Jew or non-Jew, or to mislead anyone in
any way whatsoever.

"You shall not deal falsely, nor lie to one another."

(Leviticus 19, 11)[11]

Mind-Stealing

This law also forbids all hypocrisy or flattery by which
we seek to gain the good opinion of others in order to
get the better of them. Deception of this sort is called
"stealing the mind." The man who commits this
wrong is making his way into the mind of his fellow
just as a thief would sneak into his house to carry away
something for himself.

This crime is practised in our days on a fairly large
scale. We all know, or have heard, of confidence
tricksters, and dishonest advertisers who indulge in
"stealing the minds" of men. These people do not
know what it means to respect the feelings of their
fellow men, otherwise they would not stoop to such
mean practices. But whatever others may do, for the
Jew his duty is clear. He must remember that all
"mind-stealing" is not only dishonourable in itself,
but is also a betrayal of the honour of Israel which
every Son of Israel has in his keeping.

"The remnant of Israel shall do no iniquity nor speak lies, neither shall a deceitful tongue be found in their lips" (Zephaniah 3, 13).[12]

(iv) ILL-WILL

Respect for the feelings of others demands that we shall bear no ill-will towards our fellow man. To bear ill-will towards someone, means that we wish him harm, and this may even tempt us to harm him ourselves. It is therefore our duty to suppress all feelings of hatred against any man. As we shall see, all men are, after all, brothers; and it is only right to expect that brothers shall have no feelings of hatred towards one another.

"You shall not hate your brother in your heart" (Leviticus 19, 17).[13]

Vengeance

The demand that we should not bear any ill-will against our fellow man forbids all revenge. Of course, if a man has, for example, wronged us by injuring our person or property, it is only right that we should see that he pays the penalty. This is necessary not only in order that we may be compensated for the damage done to us. He must be punished so that he may not go on injuring others. But this penalty must be inflicted on him in a spirit of justice, not out of a sense of revenge. As we are not the best judges in matters

which concern ourselves, we certainly are not allowed
to take the law into our own hands. We have to bring
him to the Court, where he will receive punishment
according to what he deserves. Once he has paid the
penalty for his offence, we must forget all about it.

Hatred of Enemies

The teachers of the Jewish religion took a very severe
view of hatred. "Whosoever hates *any man*," they
declared, "hates the Creator of all things." "*Any
man*," that is, whether Jew or non-Jew. They thus leave
us no loophole to suppose that we may hate those who
do not happen to be related to us by ties of religion.
Nor did the Jewish religion ever make a distinction in
this matter between friend and enemy. The statement
that the Hebrew Bible bids us to hate our enemies is
a lie. Anyone who is familiar with our Scriptures will
be able to lay his finger on a number of passages
where we are commanded to be gentle and considerate
even to those who have wronged us. As an example,
we may recall the declaration of Job:

"I should have denied God that is above, if I
rejoiced at the destruction of him that hated me, or
exulted when evil overtook him" (Job 31, 28–29).

The only people we may hate and at whose down-
fall we may rejoice are the enemies of God and man.

To be too sentimental about them, and to seek to spare them, is to hate both God and men. But, apart from these criminals against human society, we must not allow our particular likes or dislikes to interfere with the command of the Jewish religion neither to hate nor bear ill-will against any man. And here too, as in all other demands of Justice, the test is ever the same: "What is hateful to you, do not do unto others."

Chapter III

THE SECOND STEP—RIGHTEOUSNESS

The More Difficult Step

The next step leading to a good life is Righteousness.
In Hebrew it is called *Zedakah*.

Righteousness is a more difficult step to master than
Justice. All that Justice demands of us, as we have
seen, is that we do no harm to others. Righteousness
comes to us with a further demand. It asks us also to
do good to others. Justice teaches that we may *not do*
unto others what is hateful to us; Righteousness teaches
that we should *do* unto others what we would like to
have done to ourselves.

The Machine of Human Society

You will remember how we compared human society
to a machine. This comparison will be found helpful
when we try to understand clearly the difference
between Justice and Righteousness. Justice forbids us
to interfere with the smooth working of the machinery
of human society; Righteousness orders us to help to
make it work properly. But no machine can work

properly if one of its cogs, wheels or belts slackens and refuses to function. It is the same with the machine of human society. Only if each human being, who forms a part of this machine, does his bit, can it be made to run smoothly and well. This, of course, requires of each one of us special exertion and effort; but no man can claim to be a good man, unless he is prepared to play his part, as Righteousness demands of him.

Rescuing our Fellow-Man from Danger

Like Justice, Righteousness is concerned with the life, property, and feelings of others. But, coming with its further demand, it imposes on us a corresponding set of commands and duties.

In its concern for the life of others, Righteousness commands that we should not stand idly by when life or health is in danger.

"You shall not stand idly by the blood of your neighbour" (Leviticus 19, 16).[1]

It is therefore our duty, when we see a human being in peril or in distress, to come to his rescue and to do everything in our power to save him. This duty overrides all other commandments of our Torah. Even the Sabbath must be broken, if necessary, in order to help a man in danger.

"The Sabbath is given to you, not you to the Sabbath" (Talmud).[2]

If a man hesitates to save the life of his fellow, because he does not want to profane the holy day of rest, he is guilty of bloodshed.

Provision of Livelihood

In its concern for the life of others, Righteousness demands that we should provide our fellow-man, whether Jew or non-Jew, with the means whereby he can make a living. Among no people of old was there so much concern shown for the livelihood of those in want as in Israel. In the ancient Hebrew State, the poor were assured of a living by the rights which the Bible gave them in the harvest. These rights were five in number:

1. They had the right to the corn standing in the corners of the field—*Peah* ("Corner").
2. They had the right to ears of corn dropped on the ground at the time of the reaping—*Leket* ("Gathering").
3. They had the right to gleanings of the vineyard—*Peret* ("Dropping").
4. They had the right to the defective clusters of grapes—*Oleloth* ("Young Clusters").
5. They had the right to the sheaf of corn forgotten in the field by the farmer—*Shikchah* ("Forgetfulness").

All these parts of the harvest belonged to the poor. The farmer was not allowed to gather them; and all needy people—the poor, the widow, the fatherless as well as the non-Jewish stranger—were equally entitled to benefit from them.

In addition there was a poor tax, known as *Maaser Oni*, "Poor Tithe." Every third year, the Jewish farmer had to set aside a tenth of his produce and take it to a special storehouse in his district, where the Poor Tithe was received for distribution among the needy.

The Divine Owner

All these rights of the poor in the produce of the soil were based on the teaching of the Jewish religion that whatever we have belongs to God. God is the owner of the world and all that is therein.

"The earth is the Lord's and the fulness thereof"
(Psalm 24, 1).[3]

God is thus the real landlord. We are only His tenants. In order to enforce this important teaching, the Torah ordained the *Shemittah*, the sabbatical year. Every seventh year the land had to rest. It was to be "a year of solemn rest for the land unto the Lord." In that year the Jewish farmer had to give back to its Divine Owner the land which he held from Him as tenant. He was therefore forbidden to cultivate it, or to harvest its produce for his own exclusive use. The land belongs to all God's creatures, and everyone has the right to enjoy its produce and eat its fruit.

As God's tenants, what we have we hold from Him, on condition that we pay Him His due. This must be paid in the form of assistance to those who through misfortune have been deprived of their share in God's world. If we fail in this duty, we not only rob the poor of their right, but also, so to speak, rob God of His due.

Charity

In olden times the Jew was able to discharge his duty towards the needy by leaving them their share in the produce of the land. When the Jewish people lost their ancestral soil, these particular rights were lost to the poor; but their right to be helped to make a living remained as binding as ever. We owe it to them for the same reason as the Jewish farmer of old owed to the needy a share of his produce. All we have is the Lord's. It is one and the same thing whether we have produce or money. Everything belongs to God.

"Mine is the silver, and mine is the gold, saith the Lord of Hosts" (Haggai 2, 8).[4]

Righteousness therefore demands that we give up a part of our possessions for the support of those in want. Support of the needy generally goes by the name Charity, which means kindliness; in Hebrew, however, it is called *Zedakah*, Righteousness. Support of the poor, as the Jewish religion understands it, is not merely an act of kindliness. It is a simple act of Righteousness, which we must carry out in fulfilment of our duty both to God and to those in need. As the needy are many and the demand is continuous, Charity becomes one of the regular duties of our daily life.

Charity can be performed in many ways:

(i) By giving money to the begging poor.
(ii) By feeding the hungry.
(iii) By clothing the naked.
(iv) By giving hospitality to the wayfarer.

"Is it not to deal your bread to the hungry, and that you bring the poor that are cast out into your house? When you see the naked, that you cover him, and that you do not hide yourself from your own flesh" (Isaiah 58, 7).[5]

The righteous Jew will at all times thus assist those in need. Moreover, in accordance with the teachings of his religion, he will make no distinction in his charitable work between Jew and non-Jew. He will offer help to all in want, of whatever nationality or religion. He will also assist even his personal enemy, as is required by his religion. Moreover, even if he himself is poor, he will make it his duty, as far as he is able, to help those who are in greater distress than himself. He will in addition, keep his door ever open to the vagrant poor, and the wandering stranger, and offer them food and shelter.

Concern for the Feelings of the Poor

In giving Charity to the poor, Righteousness commands us to show concern for their feelings. The giver must not subject the poor man who comes to him for help to any indignity or insult. He dare not hurt his feelings in any way, or reproach him with laziness. He must remember that very few people indeed take easily to begging. To most people begging comes as an ordeal, to which they are driven by a society which can find no work for them. There are, of course, imposters and loafers: and individuals such as these must not be encouraged. But the majority of people prefer work to a life of beggary: and if they do go about begging, the fault is not theirs, but that of society. These are truths which Righteousness commands every giver of charity to remember. Bearing these facts in mind, he will treat the poor with sympathy and consideration, and speak kindly to them. Kind words may in fact cheer the heart of the depressed poor more than a gift. On the other hand, to give generously with a sullen look is to rob the deed of much of its value.

"Lo, is not a word better than a gift? But both are with a righteous man" (Ben Sira 18, 19).

The Highest Form of Charity

But that is not all. Righteousness, in its concern for the livelihood and feelings of others, bids us to remove, as far as we can, the causes that make it necessary for the poor man to beg at all. This we can do by helping him in his endeavour to earn a livelihood. There are several ways in which we can give him such assistance. We may either give him employment; or we may offer him a loan to enable him to buy tools with which to work, or goods with which to trade. Such assistance is considered by the Jewish religion as the highest form of charity; and it is expressly commanded in the Torah as one of our duties towards the poor:

"If your brother becomes poor and his hand fails with you, then shall you uphold him, though he be a stranger or a sojourner with you." (Leviticus 25, 35)[6]

The Torah, furthermore, forbids demanding interest on a loan to the poor man:

"You shall not take of him usury or increase . . . that your brother shall live with you" (Leviticus 25, 36).[7]

To demand interest from a poor man, who is struggling to make a living and at the same time to repay his debts, is to make it very hard for him to maintain himself.

It will be seen that here too, the Jewish religion, in

its concern for the livelihood and feelings of those in need, includes the non-Jew, described in the Bible as "stranger or sojourner". The non-Jew in difficulty must also be helped with a loan; and also from him it is forbidden to take interest. This is the duty which Righteousness, as taught by the Jewish religion, places upon the Jew; and it is a duty which no righteous Jew will seek to evade.

False Charity

Charity as an act of Righteousness must not contain any shred of unrighteousness. Any charity which is not free from such a blemish is false charity. It is, for example, false charity to rob one person in order to relieve another.

"If a man steals with one hand, and gives charity with the other hand, he will not be acquitted in the hereafter" (Talmud).

It is likewise false charity to help the poor, while not repaying one's debts, or not paying proper wages to workmen. Charity given in righteousness is praiseworthy; but what is given at the expense of what is right and just is not charity.

Concern for the Property of Others

In its concern for the property of others, Righteousness commands us to protect the belongings of our fellow-man from loss. Examples of this duty are to be found in the Biblical law, which requires us to restore lost articles to their owners, and to help a man struggling to load or unload his beast.

"If you meet your enemy's ox or his ass going astray, you must surely bring it back to him again" (Exodus 23, 4).

"If you see the ass of a man who hates you lying under its load, you must not pass by him, but you must help him to release it" (Exodus 23, 5).

Here we find laid down the duty of restoring and rescuing the property of our fellow-man, a duty which Righteousness commands us to perform even towards a personal enemy. And what is said of lost property and the fallen beast of burden applies to any loss or danger to which anything belonging to our neighbour is exposed. In every case we must not pass by it, but do what we can to save it.

Righteousness Towards Animals

Righteousness, as a standard of conduct, knows of no exceptions. It includes all living creatures, animals no less than human beings, This was so from the earliest days of the Jewish religion. At a time when to speak of Righteousness towards a fellow-man seemed ridiculous, the Jewish religion did not hesitate to demand it even for animals. Indeed, consideration for the beast was always regarded among the Jewish people as the mark of the righteous man:

"The righteous man regards the life of his beast"
(Proverbs 12, 10).*

In its concern for animals, Righteousness demands that we should consider their needs and feelings in every possible way. It forbids cruelty to animals, and imposes upon us a number of duties which we must observe towards them.

Among the teachings of the Jewish religion regarding the treatment of animals, the following may be mentioned.

1. The animal fallen by the way must be raised with the same care as if it were a human being.
2. The animal, whilst employed in treading out the corn, may not be muzzled, but must be allowed to eat freely from the grain.
3. Animals of different species, as for example an ox and an ass, must not be yoked together for work. As they differ in nature and strength, it is cruel to force them to work together under one yoke.
4. Animals must be allowed to rest from working on the Sabbath day, just as the owner himself has to rest.

5. We are forbidden to sit down to a meal before feeding our animals, or domestic pets.
6. We are forbidden to lay upon an animal a burden heavier than it can stand.
7. We are forbidden to strike an animal unnecessarily.
8. We may not buy any animal or bird, unless we can provide enough food for it.
9. Killing animals or birds for sport is forbidden.
10. In slaughtering animals or birds for food, care must be taken not to inflict unnecessary pain. The Jewish laws of *Shechitah* have been so drawn up as to reduce to a minimum the suffering which is inevitable when meat is prepared for eating.

There are other laws in the Jewish religion for the protection of animals from cruelty. It is thanks to these laws, which the Jewish people has, on the whole, observed through all the centuries, that the Jews are to the present day distinguished for their humane treatment of animals. Jews do not indulge in killing for sport. It is therefore no wonder that it was left to a son of our people to give the main impetus towards the founding of the first Society for the Prevention of Cruelty to Animals. The name of this Jew was Lewis Gompertz (died in London in 1861). He had indeed to fight hard in order to achieve his end. On the one side, there were those who refused to admit that the treatment of animals was anybody's concern; on the other side, there were those who held that to believe that man had any duty towards brute creation was a sin. Gompertz, however, inspired by the teachings of his religion, persevered in spite of all opposition, until cruelty to animals came to be treated in all civilized countries as a punishable crime.

Righteousness Towards the Rest of Creation

Righteousness, as a standard of conduct that knows of no distinction, is also concerned with the rest of creation, besides human beings and animals. It commands us to preserve everything that can be of any use. It is therefore forbidden to destroy, damage or waste food. It is likewise forbidden to destroy or damage useful plants. Even though we ourselves may not need them, they may be of some use to other people. The destruction or unnecessary waste of anything which can be put to use, is regarded in the eyes of the Jewish religion as a sin. It is indeed a serious sin which offends against the commandment "You shall not destroy" (Deuteronomy 20, 19).[*] It is a sin against the law of Righteousness, which the Jew must obey; and it is also a sin against society, for whose welfare and interest each of its members must exert himself and work.

Chapter IV

THE THIRD STEP—LOVE

The Height of Goodness

We now come to the third and final step. Its name is Love. In Hebrew it is called *Ahavah*. More generally it is known as *Chesed*, which means "Lovingkindness," or "Grace."

Love is the height of goodness. It cannot be reached unless we have learnt thoroughly and well the lessons of Justice and Righteousness. Where there is no Justice and Righteousness, there can be no Love. But, at the same time, Love is greater than Justice and Righteousness put together. This becomes clear when we compare the meaning of Love with that of Righteousness and of Justice.

Justice demands that we do no harm to others.

Righteousness commands that we do good to others.

Love makes us *want* to do good to others.

Love has only one motto, from which all the rest follows. This motto has been proclaimed by our Torah in its command:

"THOU SHALT LOVE THY NEIGHBOUR AS THYSELF"

(Leviticus 19, 18).[1]

47

In these golden words, we have the Jewish Law of Love which bids us to do unto others what we would like to be done to ourselves.

Love and the Machine of Human Society

Here again, our illustration drawn from the machine will help to bring out clearly the distinct meaning of Love. Love does not mean that we must not interfere with the working of the machinery of human society. That is the purpose of Justice. Nor does it mean that we must help to make it work. That is the purpose of Righteousness. Love means that we should *want* to make it work. There is a world of difference between doing a thing because we *must* do it, and doing it because we *want* to do it. In the one case the work is scamped and careless; in the other the work is well done and well ordered. We know all this from our daily lives. And what is true of our everyday tasks is true of our duties towards society, and towards each of our fellowmen who make up society. Only if we do these duties with Love can we claim to fulfil them properly and well.

Deeds of Lovingkindness

There are in fact a number of duties which our religion commands us to do to our fellow-man, but which we cannot fulfil without Love. These are known as "Deeds of Lovingkindness," in Hebrew *Gemiluth Chasadim.* Charity, for example, is, strictly speaking, an act of

Righteousness. When we give a sum of money to help the poor, it often makes little difference whether we do so willingly or unwillingly. We perform an act of Righteousness, perhaps not quite in the proper way, and the poor benefit by our help; and this is what chiefly matters. But "Deeds of Lovingkindness" can be fulfilled only through Love, and are meaningless unless performed in a spirit of Love.

Special Deeds of Lovingkindness

Among the special deeds of Lovingkindness taught by the Jewish religion the following occupy an important place:

1. *Bikkur Cholim* ("Visiting the Sick"). The comfort which a visit brings to a person who is ailing, is often very great. It gives him some relief, and at times may even help him for a moment to forget his pain. To visit the sick is, therefore, one of the duties which a man whose heart is filled with lovingkindness will not fail to perform. Filled with love, he will know how to behave towards the sick man. He will not bore him with useless and wearying talk, but will speak to him words of good cheer, faith and hope. Nor will he make a difference between one man and another. He will visit all his ailing acquaintances, of every rank or class, high or low, whether Jews or non-

Jews. Furthermore, if the sick person is in need, he will make it a rule not to appear empty-handed when calling on him.

2. *Hachnasat Kallah* ("Dowering the Bride"). This has always been regarded, in the Jewish religion, as one of the greatest deeds of lovingkindness. It means, first of all, assisting a poor young couple to get married and to set up a home; and it also means helping to make a bride and bridegroom happy on the day of their wedding.

3. *Nichum Avelim* ("Comforting Mourners"). This is a deed of lovingkindness, which Love never fails to fulfil.

"Fail not to be with them that weep, and mourn with them that mourn" (Ben Sira 8, 31).

A man who has feelings of Love will know how to relieve the grief of mourners. He will express sorrow for their loss, and will speak words of sympathy and comfort.

Love and Our Own Rights

Love also means giving up our own rights sometimes in favour of people who are in a less fortunate position than we are. We stand, for example, in a queue on a cold wintry day; and we see a poor man, ill-clad and shivering, standing behind us. It is an act of love to change places with him. We are of course within our rights if we retain our place; but, if we are filled with Love, we shall willingly allow him to be attended to first. The teachers of the Jewish religion have a special name for this kind of loving act. They call it *Li-fenim mi-shurath ha-din*, "withdrawing from the line (which is ours) by right." Once we act in this way and cease always to insist on what we are strictly entitled to, we live according to the Jewish law of Love. This does not mean that we need love others more than ourselves; but it does mean that we are prepared to help them, even at the cost of a sacrifice to ourselves.

General Acts of Love
There are other acts of Love which the Jewish religion stresses. A man filled with Love will not only avoid quarrels, but will try, wherever he can, to establish peace and goodwill. He will *think* kindly of others. If someone offends him, he will reprove him gently, and will readily forgive and forget the offence. He will be courteous and patient; and he will receive every person, in the words of our ancient teachers, "with a cheerful countenance."

Meaning of "Love your Neighbour"
We can now understand what our Torah means in wanting us to love our neighbour. It does not mean that we should feel fond of him, or that we should find him attractive. That would be against the spirit of the

Jewish religion, which never asks for the impossible. There are a number of people, whom, with the best will in the world, we cannot like. There are unpleasant people, from whom we had better keep away; unfriendly people, with whom we cannot be friendly. But it is possible and right that we should help and be willing to help a man, even though he himself may not be particularly to our liking. This is what is meant by loving our neighbour; loving to stand by him when he needs us; not feeling fond of him or thinking he is nice when he isn't.

Who is Our Neighbour?

Yet the word neighbour does not include everyone. There are some people whom we may not love. There are some criminally-minded people, cruel people, whom to help is to encourage in a life of dishonesty and wickedness. They are not the type of neighbour we have to love. A neighbour is a man who behaves towards society in a decent manner. This is clear from the Hebrew word *Rea*, used by the Torah in connection with its Law of Love. The word *Rea*, generally translated "neighbour," really means a fellow, a companion, a person who joins us for some common purpose. This common purpose is to keep the machine of human society in proper running order. A man who makes it his business to throw spanners in this machine is not our fellow. Once, however, a man acts as a decent member of society we have to love him. He need not be our next door neighbour, nor need he be related to us by ties of blood or religion. He is our fellow, and entitled to our love.

Brotherhood of Man

This command to love our fellow, whoever he may be, is based on the Jewish teaching of the Brotherhood of Man. Judaism was the first religion to teach that all men are brothers, all children of One Father in Heaven, Who made every one of us:

"Have we not all One Father?
Has not One God created us?" (Malachi 2, 10)[2]

As children of one divine family, we must love all our brothers and sisters everywhere, and show this love of ours by helping lovingly those in need of us.

Love of the Stranger

While Jewish Love makes no distinction between one man and another, and wants us to help anybody in need, it stresses particularly the love of the "stranger."

"The stranger who dwells with you, shall be unto you as one born among you, and you shall love him as yourself" (Leviticus 19, 34).[3]

The "stranger" is a person of another country or another religion, who comes to stay with us for a shorter or longer while. He is more or less a "refugee." He is poor and in need. He cannot be dismissed with some casual relief, but may require *constant* help. He may thus become a burden to us. Nevertheless, the Torah teaches us to treat him all the time with brotherly love. He must be given a chance to make a living and must enjoy full equality in the eyes of the law with every other citizen.

> "One law and one ordinance shall be for you and for the stranger that sojourns with you"
>
> (Numbers 15, 16).[4]

Such, in brief, are some of the details of the law of Love, which the Jewish religion taught as far back as four thousand years ago, and which the world at large has, as yet, hardly begun to learn or understand. All the more is it the duty of the Jew to set an example in true human love; and, in obedience to his religion, make no distinction between one man and another, but treat all decent human beings alike as brothers and sisters, as children of One Father in Heaven.

Chapter V

LEARNING THE STEPS

The True Son of Israel

We have examined the lessons in good behaviour taught by the Jewish religion. We have seen that these lessons consist of three steps: namely, Justice, Righteousness, and Love. A Jew who has mastered these steps is just, honest, helpful, kind, and loving. He is the real Jew, a true son of Israel, the people in whom "God is glorified."

"And He said to me: 'Thou art My servant, Israel, in whom I am glorified'" (Isaiah 49, 3).[1]

The Good Pupil

But it is one thing to teach a lesson, and another to learn it. No one can be a good pupil unless he is willing and prepared to learn. He must not be lazy or playful; and he must be keen and patient. And what is true of many other difficult lessons in life, applies to the lessons in good behaviour taught by our religion. It is only if we make and keep our minds and spirits fit, that we can prove apt pupils and learn these lessons with good results.

How to Make and Keep the Mind Fit

In order to make and keep the mind fit, we must do two things. First, we must get rid of all the bad qualities—vices and bad habits—within us. They are the greatest enemies to a life of goodness. This, of course, calls for a fight with our inner selves. It is by no means an easy fight; but it is a fight worth while.

"When the fight begins within himself
A man's worth something" (Robert Browning).

Second, having got rid of our inner enemies, we must seek friends and allies. These are good qualities and good habits. They will help to keep our mind clear, active, and strong, and enable us to learn the lessons of our religion thoroughly and well.

The Enemies

The three chief enemies within us which we have to fight, are Envy, Greed and Pride. They are the three vices which cause much of the trouble and mischief in the world. They eat away character, destroy usefulness, and make the man who is ruled by them a danger to society.

"Envy, Greed and Pride drive a man out of the world" (Ethics of the Fathers 4, 28).[2]

Envy

Envy is a terrible vice. Many of the crimes people commit have their beginnings in Envy. A man sees another
person in possession of something which he himself
would like to have. He is moved by Envy. Envy eats
into his soul. He is pained. He imagines that it is his
fellow man who is the cause of his pain. He thus begins
to hate him, and in the end will not hesitate to harm
him. History is full of crimes that have been the result
of envy. Envy led Cain to kill his brother; and Envy is
responsible for a large proportion of the robberies and
murders of which we read in newspapers.

Greed

While Envy is pained at the good fortune of *others*,
Greed is dissatisfied with *self.* The greedy man is never
happy, never contented. He always keeps on wanting
more. What he sees, he wants. What he wants, he must
have. As soon as he gets one thing, he wants something
else. The greedy man is a useless man. He thinks too
much of his own needs to give a thought to the needs
of others. He is mean and miserly. He loves what he
has too much to part with some of it in favour of other
people.

Pride

Pride means regarding oneself as more important than
other people. The proud man thinks that everybody is

here to attend to his needs. He likes to order people about but he does not like to take orders. He is conceited and vain. He likes to attract attention, and is annoyed and angry if people take no notice of him. Among ordinary people, the proud man becomes a bully; among the ruling class, he becomes a tyrant. The proud man is thus a danger to society. Many indeed are the miseries which proud men have caused to mankind. The war of 1939–1945 which cost the world about forty million victims, was brought about by the horrible pride of one man, which infected a whole nation, and led them to believe that they were the master race, the *Herrenvolk*, who had to rule the world.

The Fight

Envy, Greed, and Pride, as we have seen, are the three chief enemies within us. They dwell within our hearts. They are like dirt in the works of a clock. As long as the dirt is there, nothing we do will keep the clock going right. We may wind it up regularly; we may keep on tapping it; we may keep putting the hands right—it will all be useless. It is much the same with our mind. All the teaching and learning in the world will not make us do what is just, right, and kind, as long as these mischief-makers are allowed to remain within us. It is therefore our duty to destroy these inner enemies. We must declare war against them; and we must fight them with all our might. It is by no means an easy fight. It demands of us courage, self-mastery, and self-control. But with all the difficulties of the battle, victory is essential for the sake of our character and usefulness. If we do not gain victory over these inner foes of all that is decent and good in life, they will one day master and destroy us.

True Victory

But merely to destroy these inner enemies is not to win real victory. It may, perhaps, not be too hard to get rid of Envy, Greed, and Pride. These bad qualities, after all, begin to be troublesome only when we mix with other people. We see that a man has something we haven't got, and we are envious. We see nice things, and we feel greedy. We occupy a position of importance, and we are filled with arrogant pride. Once we keep away from people, and mix with them as little as possible, these bad qualities are liable to disappear. This, of course, may be good up to a point. A man who has conquered Envy, Greed, and Pride in this way will do no harm to others. He will fulfil in every way the demands of Justice. He will, in a sense, be a good and harmless man; but he will not be a useful man. He will still have left undone the commands of Righteousness, and the requirements of Love. He will certainly not be able to claim to lead the good life called for by the

Jewish religion; and he will be a long way from true victory. True victory, as Judaism understands it, means not only *being good*, but also *doing good*. Not to do evil is not enough; it is also necessary to do good.

"Depart from evil, and do good" (Psalm 34, 15).[3]

The Greatest Danger

True victory thus requires that we should mix freely with our fellow men, be active in society, and play our part in the rough and tumble of life. It is this which makes victory rather hard to attain. It means that in addition to the enemies within, there are evils outside ourselves which we must conquer. These are the evils in society. At all times, in every society, there has been a large number of bad people. Even today, we see everywhere about us people doing things which are wrong, people who pay no heed to the demands of Justice or to the commands of Righteousness, and much less to the requirements of Love. To live a good life in such surroundings as these is indeed very difficult. To refuse to follow the evil example of others often means becoming unpopular and even hated. There is thus a great temptation to follow the crowd, and to do what everybody seems to be doing. Moreover, the fact that certain evil things are practised by society at large may lead us to think that there is nothing wrong in them.

And therein lies the greatest danger. It is against this danger that the Jew has been warned from the earliest days in his history in the words of the Bible:

"Thou shalt not follow a multitude to do evil"
(Exodus 23, 2).[4]

And it is this danger which must be fought with all the strength we can muster, if true victory is to be ours. For this battle, however, we need allies and friends to help us. These friends are the good qualities. Good qualities are like oil which is put in the works of a rusty clock, after the inside has been cleaned out. They serve to keep us going right, and to make us lead a good Jewish life, as is required of us.

The Friends

Among the most helpful of friends is the quality of Contentment. Contentment means being satisfied with one's own lot. The contented man is a truly rich man.

"Who is rich? He who is contented with his lot."
(Ethics of the Fathers 4, 1).[5]

A contented man will be neither envious nor greedy. Whether he has much or little, he will not grumble. Much less will he begrudge others any good they may enjoy. His happy disposition will make him pleasant company; and his cheerful presence will often serve as a tonic to those who are downcast or depressed.

Another most helpful friend is Humility. Humility means knowing one's true worth. It does not mean that a man should be insincere and tell people that he is nobody. A humble man is one who knows his own failings, and, at the same time, knows how to appreciate the merits of others. A humble person does not put on airs; and avoids all tricks of manner and speech that make people think he is what he is not.

The Greatest of Friends

The greatest of all friends is *Faith*. Faith is that quality which makes man put all his trust in God. The man of Faith feels that he is under the watchful care of God; and that it is God Who orders his life, and Who in the end arranges all things for him. That does not mean that he may sit with hands folded and leave everything to God. He knows that this is not the way God works. God wants man to do his bit; and, after having done all he can, to leave the rest to Him. But the knowledge that God cares for him and is concerned for his welfare, gives the man of faith a feeling of confidence of which nothing in the world can rob him. Whether in joy or in sorrow, he will always thank God, and declare, "What God does is for the best." (Talmud)[6]

A man of true faith is therefore a contented man. He

will be neither envious nor greedy, nor will he com-
plain or grumble.

A man of faith is also a humble man. The knowledge that it is God Who orders his life and that without Him man is helpless, results in an unassuming
bearing and in humility.

A man of true faith will therefore hate pride, avoid
vanity, and strive in all things for simplicity and
modesty.

The Greatest Thing in the World

Contentment and Humility are not the only gifts which
Faith brings to our help. There is something vastly
more important, which comes to us with Faith, in fact
the greatest thing in the world—the love of God. The
man who has true Faith in God will not only fear Him.
and shrink from evil doing, but he will also be filled
with Love for Him because of His care and goodness.
This Love we can show only by doing what God wants
us to do, what He commands us to do. Among the
greatest commandments He gave us is the law of loving
our neighbour. If we love God whole-heartedly, we
shall love our fellow man, whom He commanded us to
love. But where there is no such love of God, there can
be no real love for man. This is a truth which our
religion proclaimed almost four thousand years ago, but
which the world at large continues to ignore. It is there-

fore not to be wondered at that there is so little love among the peoples of the earth, and that everywhere we see hatred and strife, feuds and war. But whatever others may think, or believe, for us as Jews our duty is clear. It is to link the love of our fellow man with the love of God, and point out to mankind the golden words inscribed in our Torah:

"THOU SHALT LOVE THY NEIGHBOUR AS THYSELF: I AM THE LORD" (Leviticus 19, 18).[7]

Chapter VI

THE GOAL—HOLINESS

The Highest Perfection

True victory over the enemies within, and the enemies without, results in Holiness. In Hebrew this is called *Kedushah*. The word *Kedushah* really means "separation," a separation, that is to say, from all the evils within and outside ourselves; and in this separation lies true victory.

Holiness is the highest perfection a man can attain in life, and it is the goal of all the lessons in good conduct taught by the Jewish religion. It is the sum total of all good qualities and good standards of behaviour. It means real Faith, with all the excellent fruits of real Faith—Love and Fear of God, Humility, and Contentment; and it also means Justice, Righteousness, and Love—all these things put together. This makes Holiness the ideal which the Jewish religion sets before us:

"You shall be holy, for I the Lord your God am Holy" (Leviticus 19, 2).[1]

The Holy Man-in-the-Street

Generally when we speak nowadays of Holiness we understand by it a life given up to prayer, worship, and religious devotion. Whilst these things are essential to Holiness, they do not make up the whole of the ideal of Holiness as taught by the Jewish religion. If you study carefully the nineteenth chapter of Leviticus, where many of the most important laws of Holiness are set down, you will find that the command to be Holy is there addressed not to rabbis and others whom today we single out as holy men, but to the ordinary man-in-the-street, the farmer, the shopkeeper, the employer, and to all other people on their daily round. The farmer is commanded to act in a holy manner and leave part of the harvest to the poor; the shopkeeper is commanded to act in a holy manner, and give his customers right weight and right measure; the employer is commanded to act in a holy manner, and pay proper wages to his workmen; and every person is commanded to act in a holy manner and love his neighbour as himself. There may perhaps be only a little Holiness in these things; yet in a society in which the needs of the poor and the weak are ignored, and in which fraud is common, and hatred fashionable, it is an act of Holiness to separate oneself from the crowd and to live in accordance with these commands. There are many other commands which must be ful-

filled in order to attain Holiness, but each one of them
is within the reach of the ordinary man and woman.
In fact most of them cannot be fulfilled except by those
who take part in the normal activities of daily life.

Holiness of Work

The normal activities of life cannot be carried on without work. Holiness therefore demands that we should
work. Work is a holy duty.

> "Six days shall you labour and do all your work"
> (Exodus 20, 9).[2]

God made the world, and He gave it to man to take
care of and to develop. Man is thus expected to work,
and to work hard. He must work for many reasons. He
must work in order to make a living. He must work in
order to put his abilities to their best use. And he must
work in order to contribute his share to the welfare and
progress of the human race.

This contribution man can make whatever be his
calling. Whether he is a docker, a carpenter, a tailor,
a typist, a trader, a doctor, a teacher, a shoeblack or a
sweep, he contributes his share to the development of
God's world; and if he does his job well, he is engaged
in holy work.

The Crime of Idleness

Idleness is therefore more than a crime against society.

It is also a crime against God. No one has denounced the crime of idleness in plainer terms than have the teachers of the Jewish religion. They have declared that the lazy man is a destroyer of God's world.

"He who is slack in his work is a brother to him who is a master of destruction"   (Proverbs 18, 9).[3]

They regarded idleness as the source of many evils and as ruinous to health and general fitness. Work, on the other hand, is to them something exceedingly praiseworthy. The man who earns his living is in their eyes superior to the pious man who spends his time in idleness. Indeed, they taught that God blesses only those who in their work show themselves worthy of His blessings.

The Holiness of Pleasures

Like the world and everything else in it, our body has been made by God. He designed it; He formed it, and He gave it to us on trust. As God's property the body must be treated with care. It must be kept strong, clean and healthy. Some religions there are which treat the body as a miserable thing. Because the body has within it unhealthy impulses and evil desires, they think it must be punished like a naughty child. It must be deprived of the innocent pleasures of life, such as good food and enjoyable drinks. It must be lashed with

stripes. It must be kept dirty. There is the story of a
lady, named St. Etheldreda, who did not wash for forty
years, because she thought that this would be pleasing
to her Saviour. Now this is not the way of the Jewish
religion. The Jewish religion regards the body as a holy
instrument, which God gave to man to be used in His
service, and in the service of mankind; and it must be
treated with the respect and honour that are due to
what belongs to Him. It must not be harmed; it must
be fed, and it must be given the good things in life, to
enjoy them rightly. It is true that the body has within
it certain instincts which, if allowed to get the better of
us, can ruin our lives. But the way to overcome them is
not by punishing the body, but by controlling them and
using them to keep the body healthy, sound, and well.

Holy Living

A man who works and keeps his body in good condition in order to serve God and do good to men, lives
in Holiness. Whatever he then does, becomes an act
of Holiness. When he enjoys a good meal, he performs
an act of Holiness; when he gladdens his heart with a
cup of wine, he performs an act of Holiness. His joys
and pleasures, his leisure, his recreations, his games,
his holidays, are all acts of Holiness. They all form
part of holy living. They all help to make him fit, in
body and mind, for the tasks and duties of Holiness set

for him by the Jewish religion. They lead to that goal of Holiness to which he has been called in the command:

"You shall be holy, for I the Lord your God am Holy" (Leviticus 19, 2).

Chapter VII

THE TRAINING

The Need for Training

We have covered much ground in our search for the type of good life which is required of us by the Jewish religion. We have found that its name is Holiness, and that it cannot be attained without true victory.

But we have still not reached the end of the matter. There yet remains the question how true victory may be achieved. No soldier can be expected to fight well if he has not been given a good training. It is the same with the battle which each individual has to wage against the enemies within and the enemies without. If he is to prove a good warrior, fighting his way to victory, and through victory to Holiness, he has to go in for proper training. Without it, he will not be able to stand the strain of the fight; much less is he likely to win.

Hard and Continuous Training

For this training no half-measures will do. It must be hard and continuous. It must be hard, because the fight is a hard one; and it must be continuous, because the fight is a continuous one. Where such a training is absent, there can be no victory. This is why we see people who have the desire to lead a good life, and yet live badly. It is because they are not sufficiently trained to take up the fight, and therefore easily surrender to the enemy. They see a chance of making money in some dishonest way, and find the temptation too strong to resist. They may see the success of others, and find themselves unable to suppress feelings of envy and hatred. Or, again, they see around them many people who behave badly, and they cannot pluck up the courage not to follow their example, for fear that they may be thought different and odd. Lacking the proper training, they give way on their first contact with the enemy. They push into the background all the grand teachings about Justice, Righteousness, and Love, and ignore the call to Holiness. They thus drift into evil-doing, become victims to selfishness and other vices, and in the end ruin their own lives and the lives of others. These people have indeed lost the battle.

The Twofold Training

It will thus be clear that if we want to achieve Holiness, which simply means a good life, we must keep ourselves in good and continuous training. This training must be of two kinds, both being equally necessary.

There are things we must not do, and there are things we must do. We have only to think for a moment of the training an athlete has to undergo before he can take part in a contest. There are certain things he must not do; he must not, for example, indulge in smoking and strong drinks, and he must avoid all sorts of pleasant foods which might do harm to his constitution. And there are certain things he must do; he must take plenty of exercise, do a lot of walking, running, skipping, and other activities which will get his muscles in good trim and his body thoroughly fit.

Similarly, if we are to prove really fit for the fight, the prize of which is a good life, and a life of Holiness, we must also go in for a twofold training. This type of good and holy life, it will be remembered, makes upon us two demands: it wants us not to do evil; and it wants us to do good. Each demand requires of us a special kind of training. In order to train ourselves not to do evil, we must avoid certain things; in order to train ourselves to do good, we must continually practise certain things. Only when we combine negative and positive training, can we hope to be fit for the fight and to be rewarded with the prize of victory.

Volunteers for the Fight

This training, because it is hard and continuous, can be undertaken only by people who volunteer for the fight. It is impossible to force into training people who show no willingness. Thus it was, that when it was God's will to find a people who would enrol in the fight for goodness and Holiness, He chose the Jewish people. They alone, as we have seen, were prepared to take up the fight and endure all the hardship of the training, when all other nations refused. They were the first volunteers in the great fight for Holiness, which was begun four thousand years ago, and is still going on to the present day.

Abraham the First Volunteer

This will to fight, the Jewish people inherited from their first Patriarch, Abraham. He was the first volunteer in the fight for Holiness. He was the first to answer the call of God. Single-handed, in a world full of evil, he took up the fight for God and His way of Righteousness and Justice. Abraham thus became, in the words of the Prophet Isaiah, "the beloved of God" (Isaiah 41, 8). He became God's chosen; chosen in order that he might teach his descendants the ideals of Righteousness and Justice, and pass on to them the willingness to carry on the fight on behalf of these ideals.

"For I have known him, in order that he may command his children and his household after him, that they may keep the way of the Lord, to do righteousness and justice" (Genesis 18, 19).[1]

With this tradition inherited from their ancestors, the Jews too volunteered and also answered the call of God, made to them in the wilderness of Sinai.

"And you shall be unto me a kingdom of priests and a holy nation" (Exodus 19, 6).[2]

Israel the Holy Nation

The Holiness of the Jewish people was to consist in their being prepared to separate themselves from all evil, and to take up alone the fight for Justice and Righteousness against a world of hatred, cruelty, violence and lust. As a holy people, they were to stand up courageously to all enemies within and outside themselves, and to refuse to yield to temptations and other hostile forces that would threaten to overwhelm them. And the Jewish people obeyed the summons of God.

"And all the people answered together and said, All that the Lord hath spoken we shall do"

(Exodus 19, 8).[3]

The Lesson of Egypt

The determination of the Jewish people to become a holy nation was sharpened by their bitter sufferings in Egypt. The Egyptians were a nation which, by the standards of those days, stood at the head of civilisation. They were a highly cultured nation, skilled in all the sciences and arts then known. Egypt was the home of all wisdom of the time. Yet in spite of its greatness, it had sunk to the lowest depth of degradation and inhuman cruelty. For hundreds of years, it held in most terrible bondage a helpless people, treating them in a cruel manner, without any human feeling or pity. As long as such things could take place unchallenged, there could be no hope for humanity. And Israel alone, at that time, was prepared to take up the challenge, in order to save mankind from destruction. With this resolve, the Jewish people took their stand at the foot of Mount Sinai to receive from God the Ten Commandments for themselves, and for the whole of humanity. These Ten Commandments were the first challenge which the Jewish people hurled defiantly, in the name of God, at the nations, and their abominable ways of life. These commandments proclaimed respect for human life, upheld the right of human freedom, defended the property rights of others, and condemned, among other things, all lust and greed from which come so much of human misery and evil.

The Training of the Jewish People

But in order that the Jewish people should be fit and strong in the fight for which they had volunteered, they had to agree to keep themselves in hard and continuous training. This training was to be of the twofold kind already mentioned—negative and positive. On the one hand, they were to avoid many things which, though perhaps harmless in themselves, would tend to weaken their power of resistance in face of the enemy. On the other hand, they were to carry out a number of religious exercises, which would serve to make them more fit and eager to carry the fight on to victory.

Negative Training

Among the things which the Jew must not do are those forbidden by what are known as the Dietary Laws. There are several reasons why these laws have been given to us. Some scientists tell us that these laws are sure safeguards against diseases. They point to the fact that there is on the average a lower death rate among the Jews than among other peoples, and they maintain that this is because the Jews abstain from certain foods. While there may be some truth in this argument, that is not the reason why the Torah has ordained these laws. Wherever these laws are mentioned in the Torah, they are given under the command of Holiness. Their purpose is thus to train the Jew in Holiness. We are commanded to control our appetites in regard to certain foods which on the whole may be quite attractive and pleasant. By observing these laws we go in for a regular training in self-control, which should stand us in good stead when we are faced with temptations of all kinds. Thus we take a long step towards a life of Holiness.

Effect of the Dietary Laws

There is no doubt that the effect of the Dietary Laws upon the character of our people has been immense. They have served to teach the Jew temperance and moderation, and a self-discipline the like of which has been so rare among other peoples.

Positive Training

Among the principal things we must use as part of our training, are the *Tzitzith* and the *Tefillin*. We have been commanded to wear these as "signs" and "reminders" of our tasks and duties, and as aids to Holiness.

The *Tzitzith*, "fringes," are fastened to the four corners of an undergarment, and worn at all times. The purpose of the *Tzitzith* is to remind us to keep ourselves pure and clean.

> "You shall see it and remember all the commandments of the Lord and do them, and you shall not go about after your own heart and your own eyes after which you used to go astray"   (Numbers 15, 39.)[4]

Here we have clearly set forth the aim of this commandment. The *Tzitzith* are to help us to control ourselves when tempted by impure thoughts that may come to our mind, or by impure sights, such as nasty scenes or pictures that meet our eyes. The four fringed corners are a symbol of the four corners of the earth, filled by the presence of God. When we look at the *Tzitzith* we become mindful of His presence, from which there can be no hiding, and this should have the effect of keeping us back from any impure actions that will make us unholy.

The *Tefillin*, "ornaments," have a similar aim in view. The *Tefillin* worn on the forehead over the brain, summon us to holiness of thought, while the *Tefillin* worn on the left arm near the the heart, summon us to holiness of feeling and action.

The Biblical passages which each *Tefillin* contains bring to us a message of God's Kingship and His Providence, and a call to love Him with all our heart, soul, and might, and to observe His commandments. Thus does the regular performance of the command to wear the *Tefillin* serve to train our thoughts, feelings, and actions in the ways of Holiness.

The commands of *Tzitzith* and *Tefillin* apply only to men. Women have a special set of commandments. These centre chiefly on the home, and have as their aim the training of the woman in the divine vocation to which she has been called as a wife and mother in Israel.

Our Responsibility

There are many more things we must not do, and many
more things we must do, in order to keep in good
training. Some of these will be explained as we proceed.
This twofold training is one which no Jew has the right
to evade. It is true, as it has been said, that our people
at the very beginning *volunteered* to fight for Holiness.
But this fact does not free us from the responsibility of
carrying on the fight and the necessary training. No
soldier, once having volunteered, is permitted to stand
back; and no Jew, as a descendant of those volunteers
of old, may refuse to take his place in Israel's ancient
ranks. Our ancestors pledged their loyalty to God and
His service of Holiness, and we can find no release from
these, our ancestral obligations.

Training Still Necessary

This training is still necessary today. Some people may
tell you that man today is so much more educated than
his ancestors that he is able to lead a good life without
having to keep to this training. The best retort to such
people is the state of the world in our day. It is true
that man has made much progress since the time when
the Jews came out of Egypt. He has made many dis-
coveries and inventions, which have completely changed
the conditions of life. But has he in any way succeeded
in changing his nature? Is not man as much inclined to

violence, theft, robbery, greed, hatred, as he was four thousand years ago? If man's nature had really improved such a catastrophic war as that which from 1939 to 1945 devastated the world for almost six years could never have taken place.

Is then the training necessary today? Of course it is! There is no man, however good, who could not be made better by keeping in training; and there is no man, however bad despite this training, who would not be worse without it.

There is no question that the feelings of kindliness, pity, and mercy, which are generally acknowledged to exist in us, are due to the training to which we, as a whole, have kept throughout the centuries. This training has helped to educate the heart of the Jew, and to build up in him that humanity, that sense of Holiness, which no amount of brutality and inhumanity of treatment on the part of his enemies has been able to debase or destroy.

Chapter VIII

THE DRIVING FORCE

The Need for a Driving Force

Training is not the only condition for attaining Holiness. The best training in the world will not make of the soldier a good warrior if he does not believe in the cause for which he is fighting. It is the same with our struggle for Holiness. Our training must be supported by beliefs. Without beliefs, we shall have little desire, or feel little ability, to carry far the sacrifices which Holiness demands of us. Few people are *naturally* inclined to give up their selfish wants for the sake of others; fewer still are *naturally* disposed to love their neighbour as themselves. What we need therefore is some driving force which will impel us to do what is good, and fill us with the will to fight our way to victory. This driving force is to be found in our religious beliefs. It is these which arouse within us the urge to struggle on, and inspire us with courage to endure all for the cause of Holiness which we have been commanded to make our own.

God

The foundation of all our beliefs is the belief in the One and Only God. And when we speak of the One and Only God we think of none other than He whose name is spelt YHWH. This is the name by which He made Himself known to Moses at the Burning Bush, when He entrusted him with the mission to bring the children of Israel out of the land of Egypt; and it is with this name that He revealed Himself to our ancestors, as they stood at the foot of Mount Sinai to receive the Torah. This name which is usually translated "THE LORD", really means THE ETERNAL, who is always *there with* His people, that is to say, was, is, and always will be, with the Jewish people: He will never leave nor forsake them. He alone is thus *our* God; and it is He alone who is the one and only God, Whom we have to acknowledge, serve, love, and worship:

"HEAR, O ISRAEL, THE LORD IS OUR GOD; THE LORD IS ONE. And thou shalt love THE LORD, thy God, with all thy heart, with all thy soul, and with all thy might" (Deuteronomy, 6, 4–5).[1]

This one and only God is *ours* only in the sense that we alone of all peoples acknowledge Him, with none else beside Him; and that we alone, of all the families of the earth, have been chosen by Him for His special service. But in reality, He is the God of the whole world.

As such, we must think of Him as the Creator, the King, and the father of all mankind. These three teachings about God must always be kept together; otherwise we shall have a wrong idea of what God means to our lives.

God as Creator

When we speak of God as Creator, we think of Him as the One Who made the wonderful world, with all the beautiful things and all the marvellous creatures.

"In the beginning God created the heavens and the earth" (Genesis 1, 1).[2]

Among the works of God's creation the highest is man. Man is the most wonderful of all the wonderful things which God has made. He alone of all creatures has been made in the image of God.

"God created Man in His image" (Genesis 1, 27).[3]

Man alone, of all created things, shares something of the wisdom of God. He alone can talk; he alone can think; he alone can reason, can invent, can plan; and he alone knows the difference between good and evil. It is for this reason that God gave the world to man to take care of, and to cultivate for the good of His creation.

God as King

But the belief in God as Creator is not enough. An artist

will paint a beautiful picture, and often, after completing it, will no longer take notice of it. It is not so with the Creator, the Great Artist. He not merely created the world, and gave it to man to take care of; but He is deeply interested in the behaviour of man in the world which He has placed in his keeping.

"The Lord looks from heaven,
He beholds all the sons of men;
From the place of His habitation He looks intently
Upon all the inhabitants of the earth.
He fashioned the hearts of them all,
Who considers all their doings"

(Psalm 33, 13–15).

Thus it is that God is not only the Creator, but also the King and Ruler of the world. As King and Ruler, He has given us laws and commands which we must fulfil and obey; and as His servants and people we have to give an account to Him of the way we carry out His orders.

God as Father

A King will often order his people about simply for the purpose of showing his authority. This is not the way we must think of God. He is not only our King, but He is also our Father. His rules are not meant to make things hard for us, but to make things easy and pleasant.

They are all meant for our happiness. When a father tells his little child "You must not go near the fire", or "Look before you cross the road", it is not because he wants to make his child miserable, but because he loves him. It is the same with God. It is because He is a loving Father that He has given us laws and commands. God in His love wants the world to be a place where fathers and mothers and children can live and be happy. He has made it a bright and beautiful world and filled it with things wise and wonderful. He has also given us commandments which make human happiness possible.

Revelation

The commandments which make for human happiness, God revealed to mankind gradually through a series of revelations. In the Book of Genesis we read that God gave to Noah a number of laws, which came to be recognized as the foundation of all human conduct for all peoples and all generations. These laws which came to be known as the "Seven Precepts of the Sons of Noah" are as follows: —

1. The prohibition of idolatry.
2. The prohibition of blasphemy.
3. The prohibition of certain marriages.
4. The prohibition of murder.
5. The prohibition of theft.

6. The prohibition of eating an animal flayed alive.
7. The duty to appoint courts to administer these laws.

These laws, it will be noticed, consist mainly of "Don'ts". They only told people what not to do. As such they were but the first step leading to a good life —the step of Justice. After Noah came Abraham, to whom God revealed the next step—the step of Righteousness. After the Israelites were delivered from Egypt, God revealed to them through Moses the Ten Commandments, and the laws of Holiness in which He made known to them the third step—the step of Love —as well as the ways in which the ideals of Justice, Righteousness, and Love can be realized in their lives.

After Moses came the Prophets, Isaiah, Micah, Amos, Hosea, Jeremiah, and Ezekiel. They also had revelations from God. They were holy men through whom God communicated His will and His warnings to the people. And although they did not teach anything which can be regarded as essentially new, they each emphasized certain points in the teachings of the Jewish religion, in such a novel way as to make them bearers of new revelations.

Unwritten Torah

The Bible is the record of God's revelation. As such the Bible is known as the Written Torah. But side by side

with the Written Torah, there exists an Oral or Un-
written Torah. This Oral Torah goes back to the earliest
days, since the Written Torah was given to Israel. The
Oral Torah serves to explain the contents of the Written.
Without the Oral Torah, the Bible in many of its parts
would have been a sealed book. Who, for instance, but
for the Oral Torah, would have known what precisely
the Bible means when it orders that the corner of the
field shall be left to the poor? Or again, but for the Oral
Torah, who would have known what the Bible means
when it commands us to bind "frontlets between the
eyes"? And so on, and so forth. It is thanks to the Oral
Torah that we understand what our religion demands
of us, and that all Jews throughout the world are able
to fulfil the commands of the Jewish religion in the
same way and in the same manner. This Oral Torah,
first handed down from generation to generation by
word of mouth, was finally written down in the Mish-
nah and Talmud, and in other works that guide the Jew
in his religious life and conduct.

Messianism

The fuller Revelation that came to Israel was not intended for the welfare of the Jewish people alone. God,
as the Father of all, is interested in the happiness of all
human beings, and His laws, that make for happiness,
have been offered to all peoples and all nations. It is

true that only the Jewish people is to keep in training
for the fight for Holiness, but the aim is to win for
Holiness all the peoples of the world. Thus it was from
the very beginning, when God revealed Himself to
Abraham in Ur of the Chaldees, and invited him to
set out and conquer the world for Him and His way
of Justice and Righteousness. There He gave him the
charge to bring blessing to all the sons of men:

"And all the families of the earth shall be blessed
in thee" (Genesis 12, 3).[4]

And thus it has been throughout our history. Before
our ancestors took their stand at the foot of Mount
Sinai to receive the Law, they were invited to become
not only a holy nation but also a kingdom of priests,
acting as priests for the rest of mankind.

"And you shall be to me a kingdom of priests and
a holy nation" (Exodus 19, 6).[5]

As a holy nation they themselves were to seek to
attain Holiness; as a kingdom of priests, they were to
lead other nations to Holiness.

This duty of the Jewish people to the nations of the
world is emphasized over and over again in our Holy
Writings. Isaiah, the Prophet, in speaking of the call
made by God to Israel, reminds us of the great responsibility placed upon us as their descendants.

"I will also give you for a light of the nations.
That My salvation may be unto the end of the earth"
(Isaiah 49, 6).*

This salvation of God, reaching unto the end of the
earth, will come to pass, our Religion teaches, with
the Messianic age, which, as our Religion understands
it, is that time in history when Justice and Righteousness shall rule the earth. It is a time when nations as
well as individuals will cease to hate each other, and
will live with one another in friendliness and in peace.

How will the Messianic age come about? According
to the teaching of our religion, it will come about more
or less in a natural way. Mankind, after much suffering,
will realize that hate, injustice and unrighteousness can
only lead to increasingly destructive wars. They will
learn from bitter experience that the only remedy for
all the trouble and misery that fills the world lies in
Justice and Righteousness, practised between nation
and nation, and between individual and individual.
Among the first acts of Justice which the nations of
the world will have to perform is the restoration of the
Jewish people to their Holy Land. As a leader, chosen
by God, in this ultimate work of restoration, will be
the Messiah. He will be by no means a superhuman
being, promising things that are to come about in
another world, and leaving the present world to its
cruelties and sufferings, miseries and strife. He is to be

a man, possessed of great wisdom and piety, able to inspire the nations of the world, in common with the Jewish people, to a life of Justice and Righteousness.

The Rise of the State of Israel

We may perhaps rightly see in the tremendous happenings of our own times, the beginning of the Messianic Era. The miraculous rise of the Jewish State after two thousand years of Jewish dispersion, justifies us in the belief that what we are witnessing today is the beginning of that Messianic restoration which will finally bring about the salvation of Israel and the salvation of the whole human race. True, the end of the story is not yet. The road to full Jewish restoration is bound to be hard and stony, but the events are too wonderful to be explained except by the finger of God working in fulfilment of His Messianic promise for Israel and the whole of humanity.

The Kingdom of God

Once Justice and Righteousness are established on earth, the way will be paved for the rule of the Kingdom of God. This is a Kingdom that is founded on Love, and that can be maintained only through Love. In this Kingdom all human beings, recognizing God as Father, will love one another as brothers; Humanity will throw away all its false gods that have brought so much strife and misery into the world. All will

worship the One and Only God whom Israel has proclaimed throughout the ages, with a perfect heart. Then
shall mankind enter upon the full happiness which
God has intended for His children; and "the Lord shall
be King over all the earth; in that day shall the Lord
be one, and His name one" (Zechariah 14, 9).[7]

The Building of the Kingdom

It lies in the power of each one of us to help or to
hinder the building of the Kingdom. With every good
act we ourselves do, or by our behaviour encourage
others to do, we help in the building of the Kingdom.
With every evil act we do ourselves, or by our behaviour
encourage others to do, we hinder the building. No one
may say that he is of little importance, and that his
conduct will make not the slightest difference. In this
great work of building the Kingdom, everyone counts.
Just think of the help which every person, whatever
his ability, is expected to give in times of war. In saving
food, in raising crops, in purchasing War Savings
Certificates, there is not a person, even a child, who
cannot lend a hand, and thereby contribute to victory.
The same is true of the great fight between good and
evil in which we are all engaged. The means to serve is
given to us all, and the duty to help rests on us all. It is
only by the common efforts of all that victory can come
and that the Kingdom of God can be brought about.

The greatest share of the burden must, however, be borne by the Jewish people. As descendants of the volunteers of old in the fight for Holiness, we must take our stand in the forefront of the battle, and work even more than others for the building of the Kingdom. This we can do by maintaining the continuous training essential for Holiness, and by leading a life of Holiness. Whenever we act in a holy manner, we help greatly to bring the Kingdom into being. Our holy living cannot fail to influence the life of others for good. Just as continually falling drops of water will in the long run hollow out the hardest stone, so little acts of Holiness constantly performed will wear out all obstacles, and work themselves through to bring about the Kingdom of God. This must be our belief; this must be our conviction. "I desire to take upon myself the Yoke of the Kingdom of Heaven" is the declaration which a pious Jew makes when he is about to fulfil a command of our religion. What he means to say is "I must not merely wait till the Kingdom comes, nor only pray for it to appear, but by my own life and by my actions, such as the one I am about to perform, I must help to bring it about."

Our Privilege

We must indeed regard it as a great privilege to have been chosen by God to be the principal builders of His

Kingdom. No Jew who realizes the meaning of it all will fail to carry out the tasks placed upon him and to do his duty with love and joy. No matter how hard the trials and how terrible the odds, he will rejoice that God has deemed him worthy to call him to His service. If God seems to have stationed him where the battle is fiercest and the danger greatest, he will reflect that He would not have done so, did He not reckon him among His most valiant and faithful servants who would never desert Him and His cause. With a heart full of thankfulness he will join in the centuries-old chorus of the Jewish people, and proclaim in the words of our daily prayers:

"Happy are we; how goodly is our portion, how pleasant is our lot, and how beautiful our heritage."[8]

Our Responsibility

But this privilege carries with it great responsibilities. Because we have been entrusted with this principal share in the building of His Kingdom, our responsibility to God is all the greater. Any failure to carry out our appointed duties must bring with it punishment, just as every fulfilment of our tasks brings its reward. It is not for the Jew to pick and choose among his duties. A soldier who has been assigned to the front line may not desert his post on the excuse that he wants to act as stretcher-bearer. It is the same with us. Our duties have been well defined. They are all included under the term Holiness; and it is for us to carry them out to the best of our ability.

What kind of reward and punishment is given us for obedience or disobedience, we cannot tell. The pious Jew is satisfied to leave it to the righteous judgment and love of God. But however it may be, some of the reward and punishment is received in this world. If we disobey the will of God, we must not be surprised if things go wrong. If we do His will, He will reward us. This reward may take various forms. Sometimes it is given in the form of material blessings; at other times in the form of His loving care and protection from peril. At all times we receive it in the inward peace and joy that come from serving God and doing His will.

Immortality

The real reward or punishment, we believe, will be given us in the world to come. Life, according to the teaching of our religion, does not come to an end when the body is laid in the grave. There is in each man an immortal soul, which is left untouched by death. This immortal soul has been described in the Bible as having been breathed into us by God, and it is this immortal soul which makes man superior to all other living beings in creation.

Possessed of an immortal soul, man is the child of

eternity. The life that comes to him after death is richer and fuller than the life that ends in death. We cannot picture the life of the soul after death, any more than we can picture the life of the human soul before it entered the body. It is the one and same life. It came from God, and it goes back to God.

"The dust shall return to the earth as it was, and the spirit shall return to God who gave it"
(Ecclesiastes 12, 7).*

There in the presence of God, we shall take our stand to receive our reward or punishment. Of course, we can have little idea of what reward or punishment is like in the world to come. But we can gain some idea, if we think of the pain we feel when we realize that we have been guilty of a monstrous act; and of the satisfaction and happiness we feel when we have done something really good. Something like this, we may imagine, will be our reward and punishment in the hereafter. Stripped bare of all sham and make-believe, our souls will realize to what extent we have carried out, or failed to obey, the will of God; and according to our own verdict will be our misery and punishment, or our happiness and reward.

Having received our punishment, or entering upon our reward, we shall come into the richer and fuller life beyond. We bury a bulb in the brown earth. The bulb is not much to look at, but from it springs the fragrant tulip or hyacinth. So it is with the life after death. The life we gain is larger and richer than the life we lose. The life we begin is finer and freer than the life that came to an end. It is a life with God, Who is the source of all life.

Chapter IX

THE HOLY RALLIES

The Need for Rallies

We have learnt something of the beliefs which are the driving force of a life of Holiness. As long as we hold fast to these beliefs, nothing in the world can shake our will to fight our way through to true victory. Where, however, these beliefs fade away, there is little guarantee that the enemies within and without ourselves will not get the better of us, and bring about our surrender.

But the depressing cares of everyday life, and the unholy influences to which we are exposed in our daily contacts, often deprive these beliefs of much of their power. They either deaden their effect, or, at best, prevent us from giving them enough thought to make them the real driving force in our lives. For these reasons our Religion has set apart special days, known as "Holy Convocations," or "Assemblies." They are Holy Rallies, specially held to remind us of those grand beliefs which are to inspire us in our fight for Holiness, and to rouse us to fresh energy and enthusiasm for the struggle to which God has called us.

Character of the Holy Rallies

Of these Holy Rallies, some are connected with certain great events in Jewish History, and thus help to recall the special love shown by God to the Jewish people. Others are of a universal character; they concern, that is to say, the whole of humanity. All of them are days of rest; days on which we have to set aside our ordinary occupations and business, in order to be free to think of the beliefs of our religion, and of the duties that follow from these beliefs. Each Rally has its special observances, which serve a double purpose. They serve to stress the particular belief, or beliefs, which the Rally is meant to hold before our mind; and they also serve to drive home to us certain lessons in Holy behaviour, which we should carry forth from the Rally into the remotest corner of everyday life.

The Sabbath

At the head of these Holy Rallies is the Sabbath, the weekly Day of Rest. The Hebrew word "sabbath" means "to cease," or "to rest." The Sabbath is the day on which we must cease working, and rest from our ordinary labours. But the Sabbath does not mean merely laying down tools, and abstaining from work. The commandment reads:

"Remember the Sabbath day to *keep it holy*"
(Exodus 20, 8).[1]

This means that the Sabbath is a day to be devoted to Holiness. It is a day on which we must keep ourselves free from all workaday occupations, in order to have time to think of the ideas of Holiness and of those beliefs without which Holiness, as our religion understands it, can never be attained.

Beliefs Recalled by the Sabbath

The Bible gives two reasons for the observance of the Sabbath. In Exodus (20, 11), we are told that the Sabbath is to remind us of the Creation; in Deuteronomy (5, 15), we are told that the Sabbath is to remind us of the Exodus from Egypt.

These two reasons do not contradict each other. On the contrary, they explain and supplement each other. It is because God created the world that He is interested in what is taking place in it, as is proved by His intervention on behalf of the Jewish people in delivering them from the Egyptian bondage; and the fact that He delivered the Jewish people from the Egyptian bondage is the greatest proof that He created the world.

The Sabbath thus speaks to us of God both as Creator and King.

As a reminder of the Creation, the Sabbath speaks to us of God as the Creator of the world.

As a reminder of the Exodus, Sabbath speaks to us of God as the King of the world.

The observance of the Sabbath serves also to remind us that God is a loving Father. As a loving Father, He is interested in our rest, no less than our work. We all need a time for rest. We need it for the health of our body, and we need it for the health of our mind. As a loving Father, He has, therefore, ordered the Sabbath rest. His love, however, is not limited to the Jewish people whom He had delivered from the Egyptian slavery. As the Creator of all, He is the loving Father of all. All, therefore, who share in the work of the household, whatever their work may be, must rest. And not only human beings must rest, but also animals. They all need rest. The animals must rest to refresh their wearied bodies. They, too, are God's creatures, and objects of His love. The man-servant and maid-servant need rest also to refresh their tired minds. They, too, are human beings, and God is as concerned in their rest as He is in that of their master.

"That your man-servant and your maid-servant may rest *as well as you*" (*Deuteronomy* 5, 14).[2]

Sabbath Lessons in Holy Behaviour

Thus we see the purpose of the Holy Rally of the Sabbath. It serves to hold before our minds the principal beliefs of our religion about God; and at the same time it teaches us some lessons in holy behaviour which follow from these beliefs.

These lessons in holy behaviour are as follows:

1. No man has the right to make another person work seven days a week without a break.
2. All human beings are equal and free before God, the serving-man and serving-woman no less than the master; and they must be treated accordingly.
3. Also animals have a claim on our care and consideration.

These are lessons in holy behaviour which are impressed upon us weekly by the Sabbath rest for our guidance on the other days of the week.

The Sabbath rest is indeed one of the most precious gifts of our religion to humanity. It is Israel's Sabbath that has given rise to the Christian Sunday, and to the Moslem Friday; and has finally made all peoples realize the importance of a break in the working week for the health and happiness of a nation. "Of all divine institutions," said Lord Beaconsfield, "the most divine is that which secures a day of rest for man. I hold it to be the most valuable blessing conceded to man. It is the corner-stone of all civilization, and its removal might affect even the health of the people."

Holiness of the Sabbath

The purpose of the Sabbath is, however, not only rest. While rest is essential for the well-being of our body and our mind, it is not the be-all and end-all of the Sabbath.

Rest in itself is, in fact, not always a good thing; when rest means idleness, it is not without its dangers. "Satan," it has been said, "finds some mischief still for idle hands to do." The Sabbath, as already mentioned, has been set aside as a day to be kept holy. It is a day which gives us the opportunity to reflect on those great beliefs of our religion which inspire the will to Holiness. It is this which makes the Sabbath a day of Holiness, a Holy Rally.

As such, the Sabbath must be a day of religious activity devoted to the service of God, our Creator, our King and our Father. It must be observed as a day of prayer, worship, and religious reading and study. All these things serve to fix in our minds the great teachings about God which the Sabbath recalls, and to inspire us with the love of God and the desire to do His will in all walks of life.

The Sabbath Joy

Sabbath as a day of Holiness does not mean that we must avoid in it the holy pleasures of life, such as good food and enjoyable drinks, and other pleasant things that gladden the heart. On the contrary, the Holiness of the Sabbath demands that we should make of it a day of delight, cheerfulness, gladness and joy.

"You shall call the Sabbath a delight, the holy of the Lord; honourable" (Isaiah 58, 13).[3]

And, indeed, what a day of delight is the Sabbath properly observed! The lit candles, the blessing of the children by the father, the *Kiddush* over the wine cup, the specially prepared dishes for the three meals, the table songs—all these things, combined with the restful atmosphere, fill the Jewish home with a spirit of joy which drives away the cares and sorrows of the week, and makes of the Sabbath a symbol of Peace.

Sabbath and the Kingdom of God

As a day of joy and symbol of peace, Sabbath is a symbol of the Eternal Sabbath that is in store, in the world to come, for those who, on earth, do the will of God, and strive to lead a life of Holiness. And it is also a symbol of the joy and peace that will be the blessed lot of mankind in the Kingdom of God, when all evil shall vanish and God will be acknowledged by all as King. This is the theme of the psalms sung on welcoming the Sabbath; and it is to the building of the Kingdom that the Jewish people renew their pledge every week with the observance of the Holy Rally of the Day of Rest.

The Festive Seasons

In addition to the Sabbath, our Religion has set aside five other festive seasons which we have to observe as Holy Rallies. These are Passover (Pesach); the Feast

of Weeks (Shavuoth), the Feast of Tabernacles
(Succoth); New Year's Day (Rosh Hashanah); and the
Day of Atonement (Yom Kippur).

Like the Sabbath, they are all days of rest. But
whereas on the Sabbath rest from work is a duty in
itself, and therefore must be complete, on these other
festivals, apart from the Day of Atonement, the rest
has been commanded only in order to enable us to
observe all the better the Holy Rally. For this reason,
work connected with the preparation of food in honour
of the festival is permitted on these days.

The Three Pilgrimage Festivals

The first three of the above-named Holy Rallies are
known as the Pilgrimage Festivals. In olden days, when
Israel was in its own land, every Jew made a pilgrimage
to the Temple in Jerusalem in celebration of these
three festivals.

Like the Sabbath, these pilgrimage festivals have
two reasons for their observance. On the one hand, they
are kept in celebration of the harvest; on the other
hand, they commemorate certain important events in
our history.

As Harvest Festivals, they are connected with the
three harvesting seasons in the Holy Land: the spring
harvest, when the barley begins to ripen; the summer
harvest, when the wheat is cut; and the autumn harvest,

when all the produce of the year, from the grain fields, oliveyards and vineyards is gathered in for storing. At harvest time, the Jew is to pay homage to the power and love of God as the Giver of all good things, caring and providing for all the living creatures He has made, from human beings to animals and the tiniest insects. Each of these seasons has to be celebrated in thanksgiving to God for the gifts of the harvest.

Pesach celebrates the spring harvest.

Shavuoth celebrates the summer harvest.

Succoth celebrates the autumn harvest.

In Temple times, each festival was marked by special services in the sanctuary which served as symbols of gratitude to God.

On Pesach, a sheaf of barley (*Omer*) was offered.

On Shavuoth, there was an offering of two wheaten loaves.

On Succoth, there was a procession round the Altar with the four plants—the *Ethrog* (citron), the *Lulav* (palm-branch), *Hadas* (myrtle), and *Aravah* (willow).

After the destruction of the Temple, the old forms of the harvest celebrations came to an end. Moreover, with the Jews dispersed throughout the globe, and living in countries where the harvest seasons differ from those in the Holy Land, the real connection of these festivals with the harvest ceased. Nevertheless, the Pilgrimage Festivals continued to be observed by the

Jewish people as harvest celebrations which have lost none of their usefulness. For they served to teach them gratitude to God for all life's beauties and the bounteous gifts of Nature, as well as the duty to acknowledge by their conduct that all they had and possessed, they owed to His care and love. At the same time, the Festivals have helped to keep alive within our people the hope that the day would yet come when they would once more be able to observe their own harvests on the soil of the Holy Land, as in the days of old. As it has been well said:

"A race that persist in celebrating their vintage, although they have no fruits to gather, will regain their vineyards" (Benjamin Disraeli).

It is in this spirit that the Jewish people, throughout the thousands of years of their dispersion, have continued to observe faithfully and devoutly their ancient Harvest Festivals. When it was no longer possible to celebrate these festivals in the same way as in Temple times, they have preserved what they could of past ceremonies, and where necessary have introduced new customs as symbols of the harvest celebrations of the days of old.

Thus it is that, to the present day, between Passover and Shavuoth, we count the forty-nine days of the *Omer*.

On Shavuoth itself, in the absence of any other visible remembrance of the wheat harvest, we decorate the Synagogue with plants and flowers.

On Succoth, the Four Plants are carried in procession around the *Bimah* (Reading Desk).

To-day in Israel, with the return of many of the sons and daughters of our people to their homeland, the connection between the Harvest Festivals and Nature is becoming real once more. Already, attempts are being made to revive in symbols some of those harvest ceremonies of old. An example of this is the offering of first-fruits (*Bikkurim*). In the old days, the offering of the first-fruits began on the day after the festival of Shavuoth and continued until Chanukah. To-day, in modern Israel, on the day following the festival, first-fruits are presented to the Jewish National Fund as a contribution towards the redemption of more of Israel's soil. In this ceremony, children take a prominent part. Carrying baskets laden with produce which they themselves have grown, they join the procession formed, singing the *Bikkurim* song:

> With our baskets on our shoulders,
> And our head bedecked with flowers,
> We come from the ends of the land,
> Bringing first fruit.

From Yehuda and Galil,
From the Emek and Shomron,
Clear the way for us,
Who bring first fruit.

Smite, smite the drum,
Play, play the flute!

As commemorations of certain events in Jewish history, the pilgrimage festivals recall the great happenings in the history of the Jewish people.

Passover recalls the Exodus from Egypt.

Shavuoth recalls the Giving of the Torah.

Succoth recalls the wanderings of our ancestors in the wilderness.

Passover

Passover recalls the Exodus from Egypt, and is known as the Season of our Freedom. It falls fittingly in the spring. For what spring is to Nature, the Exodus is to the Jewish people. Spring sees the awakening of Nature to new life, after winter's sleep; and the Exodus saw the awakening of the Jewish people to new life, after the darkness of a slavery lasting for centuries. This new life was a life of freedom: freedom from slavery, freedom from tyranny, freedom from oppression.

There are several reasons why we should celebrate, year by year, the story of those far-off days.

First, it is only right that we should gratefully remember the special love which God has shown to our people in delivering them from the Egyptian bondage, and in presenting them with the precious gift of freedom. Were it not for His loving and mighty acts, the Jewish people would long ago have ceased to exist, and disappeared from the face of the earth.

Second, the keeping of Passover serves to inspire in us feelings of trust and hope in God at all times, however dangerous things may appear for us. It speaks to us of God's watchful care and protection of our people in the dark nights of the Egyptian slavery, and gives us the assurance that the "Guardian of Israel," Who has not forsaken His people in the past, will never forsake them in the future.

But, while these two reasons may concern the Jewish people only, there is a third reason, which is of interest to the whole of humanity. In keeping the festival, we bring a message of freedom and hope to all who are enslaved and oppressed. We proclaim that God, Who is the King and Ruler of the world, cannot allow tyranny to continue for ever. Sooner or later, His judgment must break the power of tyrants and oppressors, bringing deliverance and freedom to the victims of their tyranny and oppression.

These teachings and lessons of the festivals receive special emphasis in the beautiful and touching *Seder*

(Order) observed in every Jewish home on the first two
evenings of Passover. The main features of the *Seder*
are the unleavened bread, bitter herbs, and the four
cups of wine, which recall the sufferings of slavery
experienced by our ancestors in Egypt, and the joys of
the freedom conferred upon them by God. Seated at
the table, spread with these and other symbolic foods,
are the children and other members of the company,
who are led in service by the head of the family. The
youngest child asks four questions; and the answer tells
of the story of the deliverance of the past, and speaks
also of the promise of a greater deliverance in the
Messianic future, when all human beings shall be free.

Meaning of Freedom

But freedom does not mean freedom to do just what
we like. Such is the freedom of the tyrant. He enjoys
the freedom to kill, enslave and oppress. Such is also
the freedom of the jungle. There, the strong and fierce
animal roams about at large, tearing, devouring, and
doing just what it pleases. This kind of freedom is not
a blessing, worthy of celebration. The freedom, with
which Passover is associated, is freedom for all. It is a
freedom which recognizes the right of others to be free.
This means that we must put some restrictions on our
freedom, and never use it to harm others. In other

words, we must practise self-control. Where there is no self-control, men who are given freedom may feel themselves at liberty to kill and murder, and, as in fact has often happened in history, they tend themselves to become savage oppressors.

Shavuoth

True freedom can, however, be found only in the acceptance of some kind of bondage. This may appear a startling statement; but it is true of whatever thing we may wish to do. A musician must submit to the laws of harmony, if he wants to be free to rejoice in his lovely world of music. A builder must obey the law of gravity, if he wants to be free to build a house that will stand and not collapse even before he is finished with it. And every man must become bound to some law of conduct, if he wants to be free to make of his life something noble and beautiful.

It is the same with the freedom which God gave to the Jewish people. The special love which He showed to our people in the mighty acts of the Exodus, was in order that they might be free to become unto Him "a kingdom of priests and a holy nation." This meant that they had to submit to a special kind of bondage, which would enable them to live a life of Holiness, as expected of them by God. That bondage was to be the bondage of the Torah; and it is to the Torah that the festival of Shavuoth is dedicated.

Shavuoth is the festival of Revelation. It is the anniversary of the Giving of the Law on Mount Sinai. The festival coming at the end of seven weeks after the first day of Passover, falls fittingly in the season of the wheat harvest. For what wheat is to our physical life, the Torah is to our spiritual life. They both are the principal mainstay of life. In and through the Torah, the Jewish people were to find their true freedom. In and through the Torah, they were to discover the real meaning of the freedom which they had won. The Revelation, with its gift of the Torah, thus completed the gift of freedom which was bestowed upon them at the Exodus. Shavuoth is therefore known as *Atzereth,* a word meaning "a closing"; for it is as the closing festival to Passover that Shavuoth is observed by us.

Succoth

Succoth recalls the wanderings of our ancestors in the wilderness. The festival reminds us of the loving care and protection of God that accompanied them throughout their dangerous journeys across "the great and terrible desert." (Deuteronomy 8, 15) This is brought home to us by the specially made booths in which we have to take our meals during the seven days of the festival.

"That your generations may know that I made the children of Israel to dwell in booths when I brought them out of the land of Egypt" (Leviticus 23, 43).[5]

The booths thus help to direct our minds to place our trust in God's loving care and protection, and to depend always on His goodness in all circumstances of life.

As such, the booths might well have been commanded to be erected at any time in the year. The season of the autumn harvest has, however, been specially appointed for the observance of this command, because it is at that season that the lessons of the booths are most needed. The autumn harvest is the time when the plentiful produce might fill us with a sense of pride in the work of our hands, and tempt us to put our trust in our own power and abilities rather than in God. For this reason we are commanded to take up our abode in the frail booth, and thus to remember that at all times we depend on the care and protection of God, even as our ancestors did during their forty years' wanderings in the wilderness.

As soon as the festival begins, we enter to take up our temporary residence in the *Succah*. Having learnt under its roof the lesson of dependence on God, and trust in Him, we can well give ourselves over to the joy which the ingathering of the autumn harvest brings for us.

"And you shall rejoice before the Lord your God for seven days" (Leviticus 23, 40).[6]

In this joy of the festival everybody must share. The plentiful harvest which we owe to God was not given for our own enjoyment alone. All who are in need, the poor, the stranger, the orphan and the widow, have a share in it; and they, too, must be invited to participate in our joy. This is a command of our Torah; and it is a command which is full of meaning, even in times when we have no autumn harvest of our own to celebrate. In all our joys we must be mindful of the needy and less fortunate, and not forget to include those who are to share in our happiness and good fortune.

Our Dependence on Each Other

In addition to the lesson of our dependence on God, this festival also teaches us that we all depend on one another. We all need one another; we all require the help of each other. No man can live by himself. Just think of the countless things which other people have to do for us. Just think of the many hands that have a share in providing us with the bread we eat, the clothes we wear, and the houses we live in. It is this lesson of dependence on each other which the four plants handled on the festival are also intended to impress on our minds. These four plants are taken to represent

different types of men, all banded together, all working together, all contributing, under God, their share
for the common good of society.

Succoth and Human Brotherhood

This dependence on one another is not limited to the
members of that particular society to which we, as
individuals, belong. All the nations of the world, too,
are dependent on one another, and must work together
to supply each other's needs. "When a man rises," it
has been said, "a sponge is placed in his hand by a
Pacific Islander, a cake of soap by a Frenchman, a
rough towel by a Turk, his merino underwear he takes
from the hand of a Spaniard, his linen from a Belfast
manufacturer, his outer garments from a Birmingham
weaver, his scarf from a French silk grower, his shoes
from a Brazilian grazier. At breakfast, his cup of
coffee is poured by natives of Java and Arabia, his rolls
are passed by a Kansas farmer, his beefsteak by a ranch-
man, his orange by a Florida Negro."

This interdependence of all nations means that we
all have been meant by God to live and work together
like members of one large family, in harmony, mutual
helpfulness and peace. This idea of the family of man
is another lesson of the festival of Succoth. From
earliest days the festival has been looked upon as dedicated to the idea of human brotherhood, and to the

ties that bind the Jewish people to the wide family of the human race. In Temple times already, special sacrifices were offered on the festival in atonement for the sins of the nations of the world; and the *Succah* itself has always been regarded as a symbol of the divine booth which will one day gather in all children of men as one Brotherhood, under the one Father in Heaven.

The Eighth Day of the Assembly—Shemini Atzereth

These happy days are still, however, a long way off. Neither individuals nor nations show, as yet, much sign that they have learnt the meaning of human brotherhood and the other lessons which the festival of Succoth is intended to teach. For us Jews the task however is clear. It is to remain loyal to the teachings of our Torah, which alone can keep us fit for the duties which have been laid on us. Thus Succoth is immediately followed by its closing festival, the "Eighth Day of Assembly." This is a Holy Rally specially held in order that we may dedicate ourselves anew to the service of God, and to the holy tasks that still lie ahead. With this festival is connected the celebration of the "Rejoicing of the Law" (Simchath Torah). For it is only through obedience and loyalty to the Torah that our people will be able to fulfil the great work on behalf of humanity entrusted to them by God.

The Solemn Festivals

Quite different from the pilgrimage festivals are the
New Year's Day and the Day of Atonement. Although
they are also festivals, they are solemn festivals. They
neither celebrate any event in our history, nor are they
in any way connected with the harvest of our ancestral
land. They are meant purely and simply to direct our
minds to the teachings in our religion which concern
the whole of humanity; and they are observed by us not
so much because we are members of the nation chosen
for Holiness, as because we, in common with all other
human beings, are children of God.

Rosh Hashanah

Rosh Hashanah is Israel's New Year's Day. It is, first
of all, the anniversary of the birthday of the world.
It is a festival on which we celebrate the great fact
taught in the first verse of the Bible that, "In the
beginning God created the heaven and the earth."[7]
The emphasis is on *God*. That is to say, we are bidden
to fix our attention on the truth that it is *God* who
created the world and man and everything else.

Thus, the *first* teaching to which Rosh Hashanah is
meant to direct our mind is that God is the Creator.

But to acknowledge God as the Creator, as we have
seen, is not enough. He is not only the Creator; He is

also our King and Ruler. Here we have the *second*
teaching to which the Rosh Hashanah Rally is meant
to direct our mind. On Rosh Hashanah we meet together in places of worship and proclaim God, the
Creator, as our King.

As Creator and King, God has claims upon us. He
made the world, and He made man to take care of it.
Man must therefore give an account to Him of the
way he has carried out his task. Has he made the world
into the beautiful and happy place which God intended
it to be, or into a place full of sorrow and misery? God
gave us life, and the intelligence and ability to make
good use of it; and we each have to give an account to
Him of what we have made of our lives. Have we
made of them something noble and precious, or something miserable and vile? This is the *third* teaching to
which the Rosh Hashanah Rally directs our mind. On
this day, when we celebrate the Creation of the world,
and proclaim God as our King, we have to think
of our responsibilities to God for all our failures and
sins.

But God is also a loving Father. He does not want
His children to suffer for their sins. If they have gone
wrong and astray, He gives them a chance to amend
their lives, and to make a new start. This is the *fourth*
teaching to which the Rosh Hashanah Rally directs
our mind. On Rosh Hashanah, when we are reminded

of our responsibilities to God as our Creator and King, we are also upheld by the encouraging message that, as a loving Father, He is prepared to forgive and forget, if only we try to turn over a new leaf in our lives.

Such are the teachings of Israel's New Year's Day, which give it the important place it occupies among the Holy Rallies of our Religion.

It is the Day of Judgment—*Yom ha-Din*

It is the Day of Remembrance—*Yom ha-Zikaron*

It is the Day of Blowing the Trumpet—*Yom Teruah*.

As the Day of Judgment, it calls individuals and nations to give an account before God of their actions.

As the Day of Remembrance, it calls individuals and nations to remember their misdeeds, and to examine their own conduct.

As the Day of Blowing the Trumpet, it calls individuals and nations to repentance—*Teshuvah*, that is, to return to God and to the right way of life.

For this recall to God, the *Shofar* is a most suitable instrument. It is a symbol of "the voice of the trumpet" (Exodus 19, 16), that summoned our ancestors to the foot of Mount Sinai to receive the Law of God. As such it is intended to impress upon our minds the need of obeying this Law, if we are to lead a good and orderly life, as desired by our Father and King.

The Message of Rosh Hashanah to all Mankind

As the Day of Judgment, Remembrance, and Blowing of the Trumpet, Rosh Hashanah has a message for *all* peoples. God judges all individuals and nations. He notices and punishes sin wherever it shows itself. All, therefore, need to stand in fear of His judgment, and bethink themselves of their doings and misdoings. All, must pay heed to the call made on this day, to return to God and to the way of life laid down by Him. A civilization which refuses to take notice of this call must sooner or later perish. This has been proved over and over again in history; and it has been proved again in our own times. Yet humanity will live. There will always remain a sufficient number of righteous people to save Humanity for God and His work in the world. This, too, is one of the great teachings of Rosh Hashanah. The *Shofar* is sounded not only to remind us of the Revelation at Sinai. It is also sounded as a kind of rehearsal of the blowing of the Great Trumpet with the coming of the Messiah, which will announce to the whole of mankind the end of their sufferings and the beginning of their salvation. To this grand message of Hope and Salvation which the *Shofar* brings, many of the prayers of Rosh Hashanah are dedicated. On this festival we offer special prayers for the coming of the Kingdom of God, in which "all peoples will form a single band to do the divine will, with a perfect heart."[8]

Yom Kippur

The call to repentance made on Rosh Hashanah does not end with that festival. It lasts for a period of ten days. This period, known as *Asereth Yemei Teshuvah* (The Ten Days of Repentance), ends with the Day of Atonement, Yom Kippur.

The Hebrew word *Kippur* means "wiping away," and Yom Kippur means the day on which God wipes away all our sins, and gives us a new start. For ten days we have been called by our Heavenly Father to repent and return to Him. If we answer the call on Yom Kippur, God wipes away all our sinful past, and helps us to start our life anew on a clean slate.

This answer to the call of Repentance demands of us two things. It demands that we should feel sorry for the wrong we have done. It also demands that we resolve to try to do better in the future.

As a help in this work of Repentance, we have been commanded to fast, and to deny ourselves many of the pleasures in which we indulge during the year. The whole time, apart from the sleeping hours, must be devoted to prayer, confession, and supplications for the "wiping away" of our sins, and for forgiveness. If we do our work of repentance properly, God will do His share, and grant us His forgiveness and pardon.

This does not mean that Yom Kippur is the only day on which we can repent and ask God for forgiveness.

God is our Father all the time, and not only on Yom Kippur. At any day, and at any time, if we are really sorry for our sins and repent, God will forgive us. But Yom Kippur is the day specially set aside for this work of repentance and divine forgiveness; and it is this which makes the Day the Holiest of the Holy Rallies appointed by our Religion.

For this forgiveness we need no one to help us, or to intervene on our behalf. God is the Father of all of us; and each one of us can approach Him directly. We only have to try to come back to Him, and He will take us back; just as a loving Father is only too anxious to take back his erring and straying son who feels sorry, and asks to be forgiven and re-admitted to the home.

But before God can take us back, we must make peace with His other children; in the same way as a loving father, before re-admitting his erring son, will see to it that he should first make up his quarrel with his brothers and sisters whom he happened to wrong. Otherwise his re-admission will mean more mischief and trouble in the home. And so our teachers have always insisted that, before we can hope to receive the favour of God's pardon, we must ask our fellow man to forgive us for any injury we have done to him.

But that is not all. Together with our regret for the sins done in the past year, and our resolve not to repeat them in the future, we must determine to begin a new life of justice, righteousness and love.

This is the spirit in which we have to observe the Day of Atonement; and it is in this spirit that we are reminded year by year to observe the Fast, when we read the eloquent words of the Prophet Isaiah, spoken by him, nearly three thousand years ago, at a Day of Atonement Rally.

"Is not this the fast I have chosen? to loose the bonds of wickedness, to undo the bands of the yoke, and to let the oppressed go free, and that ye break every yoke?

"Is it not to deal your bread to the hungry, and that you bring the poor that are cast out into your house? when you see the naked that you cover him, and that you hide not yourself from your own flesh?

"Then shall your light break forth as the morning, and your health shall spring forth speedily. . . .

"Then shall you call and the Lord will answer; you shall cry and He will say, 'Here am I' "

(Isaiah 58, 6–9).

Although the Day of Atonement is a day of fasting and repentance, it is not a day given over to gloom and sadness. On the contrary, it is, in a sense, a festive day, a day which brings with it the glad tidings of God's pardon and forgiveness, and the opportunity for each one of us to start a new life, without the feeling of misery for what we may have done or failed to do in the past.

The Minor Rallies

In addition to the Holy Rallies which we have been commanded to observe by the Torah, there are several other smaller rallies, which we keep in commemoration of certain events, some joyful, some sad, in our history. Each of these rallies has its special lesson to teach us, alike in matters of belief and in matters of conduct.

Purim

Purim recalls the deliverance of the Jews from the threat of destruction by Haman. It is celebrated by the reading of the scroll of Esther, and by sending presents to friends and gifts to the poor. The reading of the story of Esther serves to impress on our minds God's wonderful ways in bringing deliverance to His people, when all seemed lost. This, indeed, is an important teaching needed at all times. And the distribution of presents and gifts has also an important lesson to teach us. It is that the joy of deliverance must never be regarded as a selfish joy. We do not rejoice simply because we have been saved, but also that *others* too have been saved with us. The poor especially must be made to feel that they have a share in the deliverance. They, as is always the case, are the greatest sufferers in times of danger, and they must be our first consideration when the danger is past.

Chanukah

Chanukah celebrates the military victories of the small band of Maccabeans against the mighty armies of the Syrian king, Antiochus. But the emphasis of the celebration is not so much on the battles fought and won, as on the cause for which the Maccabean warriors entered the bitter struggle. It was in defence of our Religion, which the enemy sought to destroy. The triumph of the Maccabees was thus a triumph for our Religion, and all it means for a decent and righteous life; and it is in this spirit that the Chanukah festival is observed. Festive lights are lit in home and Synagogue, even as those victorious Maccabean heroes kindled the lights in the Temple after defeating the enemy. They are *Chanukah* Lights, lights of "Dedication," calling us to follow the splendid examples of the glorious Maccabees, in dedicating ourselves to the cause of our religion, no matter how great the odds may be against us; ever remembering that ultimate victory does not belong to the mighty in military power, or to the many in numbers, but to those who are filled with the spirit of God.

"Not by might, nor by power, but by My Spirit, saith the Lord of Hosts" (Zechariah 4, 6).°

Minor Fasts

The four minor fasts—the Fast of Gedaliah, the Tenth of Teveth, the Seventeenth of Tammuz, and the Ninth of Av—commemorating the sad events in our history, are likewise not observed merely as lamentations over past and lost glories. They all have a special lesson and message for us. In recalling, on these fasts, the various tragedies that befell our people, what we have chiefly to reflect on is the cause that brought about these tragedies. The cause was the failure of our people to live up to the ideals of Holiness for which we have been chosen. Instead of teaching the nations the ways of Justice and Righteousness, and leading them to Holiness, we became their disciples, and followed the evil examples of the heathen world about us.

"They got mixed up with the nations,
And they learnt of their works" (Psalm 106, 35).[10]

Once we think of the cause which was responsible for our disasters in the past, we shall be moved to do what we can to bring about that state of affairs which, as foretold by the prophet Zechariah, will turn our days of fast into days of feasting and joy.

"The fast of the fourth month, the fast of the fifth month, the fast of the seventh and the fast of the tenth shall become to the House of Judah days of feasting and joy *if you but love truth and peace*"

(Zechariah 8, 19).[11]

Chapter X

AT HOME AND AWAY

Behaviour at Home

Like all other training, the training in Holiness demands a training centre. It is there that we acquire the necessary knowledge and practice required to make us efficient for the daily tasks awaiting us in life.

The first training centre in Holiness is the Home. The Home is the place where we learn and practise many of the lessons in Holiness. There also we are equipped for playing our part well when we are away from home. For this reason the first command of the laws of Holiness set forth in the 19th Chapter of Leviticus concerns our behaviour at home.

"Everyone of you shall revere his mother and his father" (Leviticus 19, 3).[1]

This means that the first lesson in Holiness we have to practise is how to behave towards our parents. Our behaviour towards our parents prepares us for our behaviour in general. If our behaviour towards our parents is good, our behaviour towards God and our fellow men is also likely to be good.

128

Parents stand to their child in the place of God in many ways. They give him security; they surround him with love and care; they supply him with food, warmth and comfort. Later he comes to understand that these marvellous beings to whom he belongs, belong themselves to One Who is greater and stronger and more loving than themselves. If the child is true to his parents, it will be easier for him to be true to God; if he loves and reveres his parents, it will be easier for him to love and revere God.

On the other hand, if the child has not learnt to be respectful to his parents, he is not likely to have any respect for others; if he has not learnt to do his duty to his parents, he is not likely to do his duty to others.

Duties to Parents

It is for this reason that our Religion lays so much stress on the duties of children to parents. We are commanded not only to fear them, but also to honour them. The duty of honouring parents is indeed considered of such importance that it has been included in the Ten Commandments. And what does "honour" mean? It means more than mere obedience. It means love, affection, gratitude, considerateness and respect. It means also supporting them in their declining years; and honouring their memory when they are gone.

There is then a deeply religious purpose behind the

command to honour parents. We have, of course, to honour them, to be grateful to them, and to love and respect them for all they have done for us, for having brought to us the gift of life, and having enfolded us in their care and protection. This is more or less a natural thing, which we hardly require to be told. What the command means is that we are to honour them because it is through our behaviour towards them that we learn the first lessons in Holiness.

Responsibility of Parents

This places a great responsibility on parents. Parents must see to it that the right behaviour of their children towards them does indeed prepare them for a life of Holiness. This they can do, by themselves leading a life of Holiness and by teaching their children the ways of Holiness. Where parents fail in this duty, they cannot expect to enjoy to the full the honour due to them.

Equipment of the Home

Like every other training centre, the home must have its special equipment as part of the training it provides for Holiness in life. Chief among them is the *Mezuzah* affixed to the door-post of the main entrance into the house and that of every living room. The *Mezuzah* contains a number of passages from the Bible which speak to us of our duties as Jews. Each time we leave our home, or return to it, we are reminded of the Presence of God and of His command to think of Him and His laws at every moment of our lives, "when we sit in the house, or walk by the way, in our lying down and our rising up."

The School

Next to the Home is the Jewish Religion School. At school, we get to know more facts about our Religion and our people, and get additional training to make us ready, fit and willing to work in Holiness in all the walks of life. In school we train our mind to think, and learn to use our brains like good and sensible Jews instead of silly, ignorant muddle-heads, with no ideas and no opinions, except what we hear from others who have not the slightest notion of what our religion means, and what it stands for. There too we learn something of the great things our religion has done for us, and for the world. There we get to know something of the greatest Book in the world, our Bible; something of the great work of our Rabbis and teachers; something of our history, with all its glories and tragedies, and of the unique part which we have played and still have to play in the progress of mankind.

Such is the purpose of the Jewish Religion School as a training centre in Holiness; and the teachers who help us to acquire all this knowledge deserve our gratitude and respect. They must be treated with all the respect that is due to those who are our superiors in age, wisdom, and authority; and they must be honoured and obeyed in the same way as parents.

The Synagogue

After the Home and School have done their part of the training, we can pass on to the higher training in the Synagogue. The Synagogue is also a kind of home; it is the Home of the Community. There we meet our fellow Jews as members of the same family for common purposes. These purposes are three in number.

1. Worship—*Avodah.*
2. Study—*Torah.*
3. Practice of kindly deeds—*Gemiluth Chasadim.*

Prayer

Our Religion demands of us that we should worship God three times daily; at morning, noon, and evening.

"Evening, morning and noon I meditate and appeal, And He heard my voice" (Psalm 55, 18).[2]

This worship we owe to God for many reasons.

We must praise Him in adoration of His infinite Wisdom, Power and Love.

We must thank Him in gratitude for all the good things He lavishes on us.

It is to Him that we must appeal for help and guidance in all our needs.

In addition we must thank Him for any pleasure or good we enjoy in life, whether through food, drink, wonderful sights, or delightful odours.

But Prayer, if recited always at home, is liable to become merely a selfish thing. Selfishness, however, is never approved by our religion. For this reason we have to try to join others in prayers as often as we can.

The place best suited for this purpose is the Synagogue. It must, however, be remembered that any place is as acceptable to God as the most magnificent Synagogue. For it is not for the outside beauty of stones and bricks that God cares, but for the inner beauty of a prayerful heart.

Torah

The Synagogue is also a place where we acquire some knowledge of our Torah. The regular reading of the Torah—the Law and the Prophets—helps to bring to us the knowledge of the Torah, without which we cannot know how to lead the life of Holiness required of us.

Our knowledge of the Torah must not be restricted to what we receive in the Synagogue. The Torah is so vast, so deep, so wonderful, that we can never end the study of it. But the reading of the Law and the

Prophets in the Synagogue is a reminder that we must not make our knowledge of the Torah a selfish acquisition. We must at all times seek to share it with others.

The Practice of Kindly Deeds

The Synagogue is also a place where we are given an opportunity of practising kindly deeds. In the Synagogue we often make offerings to charity; and the Synagogue-House serves as a meeting-place where all matters for the welfare of the members and the larger community are discussed, and where plans are made for works of relief, rescue, and general social service to society.

The Trained Life

The Synagogue is thus the advanced training ground in those three great principles on which our Rabbis tell us the world stands:

"The world stands on three things: Torah, Worship, and the practice of Kindly Deeds"

(Ethics of the Fathers 1, 2).[3]

This is true of the world at large, as of the smaller Jewish world. No society can prosper, unless it makes these three principles, in a more general sense, its own:

It must know that which is good—*Torah.*

It must worship Him Who is good—*Avodah.*

It must do what is good—*Gemiluth Chasadim.*

The Jew who is well trained, and keeps himself in good training, will be fit to play his part in Holiness at home as well as away from his home and from his own community. His life will be a good Jewish life, a life marked by Holiness. He will fear and love God wholeheartedly. He will serve his people faithfully. He will treat his fellow-man lovingly. He will give of his best and noblest, to the group, borough, and state of which he is a member. He will contribute in his own measure and degree of his highest towards the betterment of mankind. He indeed will do his bit for the building of the Kingdom of God on earth. His life will have been a dedicated life, a life well spent, worthy of all the abundant goodness which God has in store for those that fear Him, and who do His will with a perfect heart.

HEBREW TEXTS

CHAPTER I

1. וְאָהַבְתָּ לְרֵעֲךָ כָּמוֹךָ (ויקרא, י״ט, י״ח).

2. דַּעֲלָךְ סָנֵי לְחַבְרָךְ לָא תַעֲבֵיד (שבת, ל״א).

CHAPTER II

1. הַמַּגְבִּיהַּ יָדוֹ עַל חֲבֵירוֹ אַף עַל פִּי שֶׁלֹּא הִכָּהוּ נִקְרָא
רָשָׁע (סנהדרין, נ״ח).

2. וְכִי־תִמְכְּרוּ מִמְכָּר לַעֲמִיתֶךָ אוֹ קָנֹה מִיַּד עֲמִיתֶךָ אַל
תּוֹנוּ אִישׁ אֶת־אָחִיו (ויקרא, כ״ה, י״ד).

3. לֹא תַעֲשׂוּ עָוֶל בַּמִּשְׁפָּט בַּמִּדָּה בַּמִּשְׁקָל וּבַמְּשׂוּרָה:
מֹאזְנֵי צֶדֶק אַבְנֵי־צֶדֶק אֵיפַת צֶדֶק וְהִין צֶדֶק יִהְיֶה
לָכֶם (ויקרא, י״ט, ל״ה-ל״ו).

4. לֹא־תָלִין פְּעֻלַּת שָׂכִיר אִתְּךָ עַד־בֹּקֶר (ויקרא, י״ט, י״ג).

5. לֹא תַעֲשֹׁק אֶת־רֵעֲךָ וְלֹא תִגְזֹל (ויקרא, י״ט, י״ג).

6. לֹוֶה רָשָׁע וְלֹא יְשַׁלֵּם (תהלים, ל״ז, כ״א).

יְהִי מָמוֹן חֲבֵרְךָ חָבִיב עָלֶיךָ כְּשֶׁלָּךְ (פרקי אבות, ב',
י"ז).

8. יְהִי כְּבוֹד חֲבֵרְךָ חָבִיב עָלֶיךָ כְּשֶׁלָּךְ (פרקי אבות,
ב', ט"ו).

9. אָבָק לְשׁוֹן הָרָע.

10. מִי־הָאִישׁ הֶחָפֵץ חַיִּים אֹהֵב יָמִים לִרְאוֹת טוֹב. נְצוֹר
לְשׁוֹנְךָ מֵרָע וּשְׂפָתֶיךָ מִדַּבֵּר מִרְמָה. (תהלים, ל"ד,
י"ג-י"ד)

11. וְלֹא־תְכַחֲשׁוּ וְלֹא־תְשַׁקְּרוּ אִישׁ בַּעֲמִיתוֹ. (ויקרא, י"ט,
י"א)

12. שְׁאֵרִית יִשְׂרָאֵל לֹא־יַעֲשׂוּ עַוְלָה וְלֹא־יְדַבְּרוּ כָזָב וְלֹא
יִמָּצֵא בְּפִיהֶם לְשׁוֹן תַּרְמִית. (צפניה, ג, י"ג)

13. לֹא־תִשְׂנָא אֶת־אָחִיךָ בִּלְבָבֶךָ (ויקרא, י"ט, י"ז)

CHAPTER III

1. לֹא תַעֲמֹד עַל־דַּם רֵעֶךָ (ויקרא, י"ט, ט"ז)

2. לָכֶם שַׁבָּת מְסוּרָה, וְאִי אַתֶּם מְסוּרִין לַשַּׁבָּת (מכילתא,
כי, תשא)

3. לה' הָאָרֶץ וּמְלוֹאָהּ (תהלים, כ"ד, א')

4. לִי הַכֶּסֶף וְלִי הַזָּהָב נְאֻם ה' צְבָאוֹת. (חגי, ב', ח')

5. הֲלוֹא פָרֹס לָרָעֵב לַחְמֶךָ וַעֲנִיִּים מְרוּדִים תָּבִיא בָיִת
כִּי־תִרְאֶה עָרֹם וְכִסִּיתוֹ וּמִבְּשָׂרְךָ לֹא תִתְעַלָּם. (ישעיה,
נ"ח, ז')

6. וְכִי־יָמוּךְ אָחִיךְ וּמָטָה יָדוֹ עִמָּךְ וְהֶחֱזַקְתָּ בּוֹ גֵּר וְתוֹשָׁב וָחַי עִמָּךְ. (ויקרא, כ״ה, ל״ה).

7. אַל־תִּקַּח מֵאִתּוֹ נֶשֶׁךְ וְתַרְבִּית . . . וְחֵי אָחִיךְ עִמָּךְ (ויקרא, כ״ה, ל״ו)

8. יוֹדֵעַ צַדִּיק נֶפֶשׁ בְּהֶמְתּוֹ (משלי, י״ב, י׳)

9. לֹא־תַשְׁחִית (דברים, כ׳, י״ט)

CHAPTER IV

1. וְאָהַבְתָּ לְרֵעֲךָ כָּמוֹךָ (ויקרא, י״ט, י״ח)

2. הֲלוֹא אָב אֶחָד לְכֻלָּנוּ, הֲלוֹא אֵל אֶחָד בְּרָאָנוּ (מלאכי, ב׳, י׳)

3. כְּאֶזְרָח מִכֶּם יִהְיֶה לָכֶם הַגֵּר הַגָּר אִתְּכֶם וְאָהַבְתָּ לוֹ כָּמוֹךָ (ויקרא, י״ט, ל״ד)

4. תּוֹרָה אַחַת וּמִשְׁפָּט אֶחָד יִהְיֶה לָכֶם וְלַגֵּר הַגָּר אִתְּכֶם (במדבר, ט״ו, ט״ז)

CHAPTER V

1. וַיֹּאמֶר לִי עַבְדִּי־אָתָּה יִשְׂרָאֵל אֲשֶׁר בְּךָ אֶתְפָּאָר (ישעיה, מ״ט, ג׳)

2. הַקִּנְאָה וְהַתַּאֲוָה וְהַכָּבוֹד מוֹצִיאִים אֶת־הָאָדָם מִן הָעוֹלָם (פרקי אבות, ד׳, כ״ח)

3. סוּר מֵרָע וַעֲשֵׂה־טוֹב (תהלים, ל״ד, ט״ו)

4. לֹא־תִהְיֶה אַחֲרֵי־רַבִּים לְרָעוֹת. (שמות, כ״ג, ב׳)

5. אֵיזֶהוּ עָשִׁיר? הַשָּׂמֵחַ בְּחֶלְקוֹ. (פרקי אבות, ד׳, א׳)

6. כָּל דְּעָבֵיד רַחֲמָנָא לְטָב עָבֵיד

7. וְאָהַבְתָּ לְרֵעֲךָ כָּמוֹךָ אֲנִי ה׳ (ויקרא, י״ט, י״ח)

CHAPTER VI

1. קְדֹשִׁים תִּהְיוּ כִּי קָדוֹשׁ אֲנִי ה׳ אֱלֹקֵיכֶם (ויקרא, י״ט, ב׳)

2. שֵׁשֶׁת יָמִים תַּעֲבֹד וְעָשִׂיתָ כָּל־מְלַאכְתֶּךָ (שמות, כ׳, ט׳)

3. גַּם מִתְרַפֶּה בִמְלַאכְתּוֹ אָח הוּא לְבַעַל מַשְׁחִית (משלי, י״ח, ט׳)

CHAPTER VII

1. כִּי יְדַעְתִּיו לְמַעַן אֲשֶׁר יְצַוֶּה אֶת־בָּנָיו וְאֶת־בֵּיתוֹ אַחֲרָיו וְשָׁמְרוּ דֶּרֶךְ ה׳ לַעֲשׂוֹת צְדָקָה וּמִשְׁפָּט (בראשית, י״ח, י״ט)

2. וְאַתֶּם תִּהְיוּ־לִי מַמְלֶכֶת כֹּהֲנִים וְגוֹי קָדוֹשׁ (שמות, י״ט, ו׳)

3. וַיַּעֲנוּ כָל־הָעָם יַחְדָּו וַיֹּאמְרוּ כֹּל אֲשֶׁר־דִּבֶּר ה׳ נַעֲשֶׂה (שמות, י״ט, ח׳)

4. ... וּרְאִיתֶם אֹתוֹ וּזְכַרְתֶּם אֶת־כָּל־מִצְוֹת ה׳ וַעֲשִׂיתֶם
אֹתָם וְלֹא־תָתוּרוּ אַחֲרֵי לְבַבְכֶם וְאַחֲרֵי עֵינֵיכֶם אֲשֶׁר־
אַתֶּם זֹנִים אַחֲרֵיהֶם (במדבר, ט״ו, ל״ט)

CHAPTER VIII

1. שְׁמַע יִשְׂרָאֵל ה׳ אֱלֹקֵינוּ ה׳ אֶחָד. וְאָהַבְתָּ אֵת ה׳
אֱלֹקֶיךָ בְּכָל־לְבָבְךָ וּבְכָל־נַפְשְׁךָ וּבְכָל־מְאֹדֶךָ.
(דברים, ו׳, ד׳־ה׳)

2. בְּרֵאשִׁית בָּרָא אֱלֹקִים אֵת הַשָּׁמַיִם וְאֵת הָאָרֶץ (בראשית,
א׳, א׳)

3. וַיִּבְרָא אֱלֹקִים אֶת הָאָדָם בְּצַלְמוֹ (בראשית, א׳, כ״ז)

4. ... וְנִבְרְכוּ בְךָ כֹּל מִשְׁפְּחֹת הָאֲדָמָה (בראשית, י״ב,
ג׳)

5. וְאַתֶּם תִּהְיוּ־לִי מַמְלֶכֶת כֹּהֲנִים וְגוֹי קָדוֹשׁ (שמות, י״ט,
ו׳)

6. ... וּנְתַתִּיךָ לְאוֹר גּוֹיִם לִהְיוֹת יְשׁוּעָתִי עַד־קְצֵה הָאָרֶץ
(ישעיה, מ״ט, ו׳)

7. וְהָיָה ה׳ לְמֶלֶךְ עַל־כָּל־הָאָרֶץ בַּיּוֹם הַהוּא יִהְיֶה ה׳
אֶחָד וּשְׁמוֹ אֶחָד (זכריה, י״ד, ט׳)

8. אַשְׁרֵינוּ מַה־טּוֹב חֶלְקֵנוּ וּמַה־נָּעִים גּוֹרָלֵנוּ וּמַה־יָּפָה
יְרֻשָּׁתֵנוּ (סדור)

9. וְיָשֹׁב הֶעָפָר עַל־הָאָרֶץ כְּשֶׁהָיָה וְהָרוּחַ תָּשׁוּב אֶל־
הָאֱלֹקִים אֲשֶׁר נְתָנָהּ (קהלת, י״ב, ז׳)

CHAPTER IX

1. זָכוֹר אֶת־יוֹם הַשַּׁבָּת לְקַדְּשׁוֹ (שמות, כ׳, ח׳)

2. ... לְמַעַן יָנוּחַ עַבְדְּךָ וַאֲמָתְךָ כָּמוֹךָ (דברים, ה׳, י״ד)

3. ...וְקָרָאתָ לַשַּׁבָּת עֹנֶג לִקְדוֹשׁ ה׳ מְכֻבָּד (ישעיה, נ״ח, י״ג)

4. סַלּוּ עַל כְּתֵפֵינוּ,
   רָאשֵׁינוּ עֲטוּרִים
   מִקְצוֹת הָאָרֶץ בָּאנוּ,
   הֵבֵאנוּ בִּכּוּרִים.
   מִיהוּדָה, מִשּׁוֹמְרוֹן,
   מִן הָעֵמֶק וְהַגָּלִיל.
   פַּנּוּ דֶרֶךְ לָנוּ;
   בִּכּוּרִים אִתָּנוּ
   הַךְ בַּתֹּף וְהַךְ בֶּחָלִיל!

5. לְמַעַן יֵדְעוּ דֹרֹתֵיכֶם כִּי בַסֻּכּוֹת הוֹשַׁבְתִּי אֶת־בְּנֵי יִשְׂרָאֵל בְּהוֹצִיאִי אוֹתָם מֵאֶרֶץ מִצְרָיִם (ויקרא, כ״ג, מ״ג)

6. ... וּשְׂמַחְתֶּם לִהְגֵי ה׳ אֱלֹקֵיכֶם שִׁבְעַת יָמִים (ויקרא, כ״ג, מ׳)

7. בְּרֵאשִׁית בָּרָא אֱלֹקִים אֵת הַשָּׁמַיִם וְאֵת הָאָרֶץ (בראשית, א׳, א׳)

8. ...וַיֵּעָשׂוּ כֻלָּם אֲגֻדָּה אַחַת לַעֲשׂוֹת רְצוֹנְךָ בְּלֵבָב שָׁלֵם.

9. ‎. . . לֹא בְחַיִל וְלֹא בְכֹחַ כִּי אִם־בְּרוּחִי אָמַר ה׳ צְבָאוֹת
‎(זכריה, ד׳, ו׳)

10. ‎וַיִּתְעָרְבוּ בַגּוֹיִם וַיִּלְמְדוּ מַעֲשֵׂיהֶם (תהלים, ק״ו, ל״ה)

11. ‎. . . צוֹם הָרְבִיעִי וְצוֹם הַחֲמִישִׁי וְצוֹם הַשְּׁבִיעִי וְצוֹם
‎הָעֲשִׂירִי יִהְיֶה לְבֵית־יְהוּדָה לְשָׂשׂוֹן וּלְשִׂמְחָה וּלְמוֹעֲדִים
‎טוֹבִים וְהָאֱמֶת וְהַשָּׁלוֹם אֱהָבוּ   (זכריה, ח׳, י״ט)

CHAPTER X

1. ‎אִישׁ אִמּוֹ וְאָבִיו תִּירָאוּ (ויקרא, י״ט, ג׳)

2. ‎עֶרֶב וָבֹקֶר וְצָהֳרַיִם אָשִׂיחָה וְאֶהֱמֶה וַיִּשְׁמַע קוֹלִי
‎(תהלים, נ״ה, י״ח)

3. ‎. . . עַל שְׁלֹשָׁה דְבָרִים הָעוֹלָם עוֹמֵד: עַל הַתּוֹרָה וְעַל
‎הָעֲבוֹדָה וְעַל גְּמִילוּת חֲסָדִים (פרקי אבות, א׳, ב׳)